TAKE THE
BULLY
BY THE HORNS

Also by Sam Horn

Tongue Fu!®
What's Holding You Back?
ConZentrate

TAKE THE
BULLY
BY THE HORNS

Stop Unethical, Uncooperative,
or Unpleasant People from
Running and Ruining Your Life

SAM HORN

ST. MARTIN'S PRESS ⚏ **NEW YORK**

The author is grateful for permission to quote from a letter by a prison inmate in the final Summary and Action Plan.

www.stmartins.com

Library of Congress Cataloging-in-Publication Data
Horn, Sam.
  Take the bully by the horns : stop unethical, uncooperative, or unpleasant people from running and ruining your life / Sam Horn.
    p.   cm.
  ISBN 0-312-27820-9
  1. Bullying. 2. Bullying—Case studies. 3. Aggressiveness. I. Title.

BF637.B85 .H67 2002
302.3'4—dc21   2002068396

ISBN 0-312-27820-9

First Edition: September 2002

10   9   8   7   6   5   4   3   2   1

Note to Reader

Dear Reader:

Please understand that because this book addresses the issue of how to deal with difficult, and potentially dangerous, people, it's important to note the following:

Accessing and using this information does not create any form of legal or professional relationship, and I, the author, my publisher, St. Martin's Press, and its employees do not accept any liability for any emotional or material loss, damage, or injury caused, or alleged to be caused, directly or indirectly, by action taken on the basis of the ideas provided. The use, misuse, understanding, or misunderstanding of the material, in whole or part, is the sole responsibility of the reader.

Please use this information in a safe and logical manner. It is best to seek independent professional counseling and legal advice if you're dealing with a challenging individual to ensure that the suggestions you receive are tailored for your specific circumstances.

Contents

Acknowledgments

"MAHALO" TO MY BRIGHT, VITAL (I'M PARTIAL) SONS, TOM AND Andrew Horn, for filling my life with love, laughter, and wonder. I am so lucky to be your mom, and I feel grateful to be part of your lives.

My sister, Cheri Grimm, continues to be the person I turn to whenever I need someone I can trust implicitly—as I do you, Sis. Thank you for running my business oh-so-effectively, and for all you do and are.

Patience comes to those who wait. My brilliant agent and editor, Laurie Liss and Jennifer Enderlin, have been waiting for this manuscript for a long time. I hope they will be rewarded for their belief in me and in this project. Heartfelt thanks for your ongoing friendship and expert guidance.

I feel privileged to know the following people. They've contributed to my life (and to this book) in so many ways, and I am enriched by their wisdom, sense of fun, integrity, positive attitude, and commitment to making a difference for others.

Judy Gray, John and Shannon Tullius, Nancy Inglis, Denise Moreland, Joel Goodman, Margie Ingram, Scott Ertl, Gar Dubois, Leslie Duvall, Rebecca Morgan, Leslie Charles, Maggie Bedrosian, Ann Petrus, Mary Loverde, Dianne Gerard, Ellen Gerrity, Dot Perry, Sandy Bremer, Sue Liebenow, Mariah Burton-Nelson, Mary Ellen Lipinski, Mary Marcdante, Karen Waggoner, Karen Danenberger, and all the Tongue Fu! Training Institute graduates.

Introduction

DO YOU WORK OR LIVE WITH SOMEONE WHO DELIGHTS IN making your life difficult? Does this person cut you down and then claim s/he was "just kidding"? Do you have to "talk on eggshells" around this individual because you never know what might trigger a tirade? Does s/he make you wrong so s/he can be right? Are you happier when you're *not* around this person?

Welcome to the bully club. This book is dedicated to people who are being or have been targeted by a bully. I hope it provides you with the confidence, clarity, and communication skills to stop bullies from compromising the quality of your life.

All the World's a Rage

The world's a stage, and most of us are woefully unrehearsed.
—SEAN O'CASEY

Bullying has become such a pervasive problem that you can't watch TV, listen to the radio, or read a newspaper without seeing or hearing yet another troubling report about the "bully epidemic." A 2001 *USA Today* column entitled "Where Have Our Manners Gone?" reported that 89 percent of Americans feel that civility has reached a new low.

Tell us something we don't know. Crowded living and working conditions have made people even more impatient and impolite. Verbal violence (*going postal, shock jocks, hostile takeovers, road rage*) is all around us. Kids on TV sitcoms curse their parents and vice versa, and we don't even blink. Game shows feature hosts who ridicule contestants—for example, "Is there no beginning to your intelligence?"—much to the laugh-out-loud delight of their approving audience.

People seem to have abandoned the Golden Rule and adopted instead "Be Cold and Rule." This observation was corroborated by a disturbing trend I have observed in recent Tongue Fu! workshops. These workshops are based on my book of that title which explains how to deal with difficult people without becoming one yourself.

Attendees would nod enthusiastically and take notes on everything that was covered. Then toward the end of the course, someone would raise his or her hand and ask rather plaintively, "I agree that these ideas work with most people most of the time, because most people care about being fair. But what if we're living or working with someone who ignores all this?"

Other participants would chime in with heartfelt amens and share disturbing stories about how someone had hounded or harassed them. All of these individuals had tried to resolve the situation amicably, to no avail, and all agreed that this one destructive individual had had a disproportionately negative impact on their life.

The participants who shared their chilling stories were for the most part quite competent in other areas of their life; however, they had not been able to keep these bullies from wreaking havoc on their peace of mind, performance, and productivity. Frustrated and intimidated, they wanted to know how they could, without abandoning their integrity, stop the insanity.

About the time these "at my wit's end" stories started cropping up in my seminars, my own "trial and terror" experience demonstrated there was a desperate need for realistic (not idealistic) ideas on what we can do if a bully decides to make us his or her target.

Been There, Done This

> I don't deserve this, but then I have arthritis,
> and I don't deserve that either.
> —JACK BENNY ACCEPTING AN AWARD

I was on a media tour when I received a phone message reporting that a family member was in the hospital. I returned home immediately and discovered shocking truths that unraveled my life and, as Russell Crowe said in the movie *Gladiator*, "unleashed hell."

The good news is, that family member has recovered completely. The bad news is, I discovered for myself what it is like to be embroiled in a battle with someone who isn't playing by the rules. I tried everything in my win-win repertoire to resolve the situation, only to have those efforts swept aside by this individual who was bent on destruction (mine).

This is a disillusioning and painful experience for anyone. It was particularly troubling for me because I'm supposed to be the queen of conflict resolution. Dozens of Fortune 500 companies have brought me in to train their employees how to turn conflict into cooperation.

You can imagine my distress when, despite my years of experience and supposed expertise, nothing I did succeeded in stopping this individual's vendetta. I didn't want to abandon the principles I espoused; however, it was obvious my ethical approach was backfiring big-time. I concluded, much to my shock and chagrin, that collaborative communication techniques *don't* work when you are dealing with people who are determined to be difficult—no matter what. I was at a total loss.

That's when I started interviewing other people who had been in similar situations. I interviewed dozens of different types of professionals to find out what they did when co-workers, clients, bosses, family members, or strangers continually crossed the line of acceptable behavior.

This book is a result of that real-life research. I promise not to waste your time on abstract theories that have no relevance in the real world. If you are dealing with someone who is doing his/her best to devastate you, it doesn't help to read a platitude that suggests you assert yourself. You want to know, "How am I supposed to assert myself? What exactly am I supposed to say? What if my response is thrown back in my face?" The specific suggestions you're about to read have been contributed by people just like you who finally figured out how to stop someone who was trying to run and ruin their life.

Read It and Reap

I read part of the book all the way through.
—SAMUEL GOLDWYN

You've heard Paul Simon's song "Fifty Ways to Leave Your Lover"? You're about to learn twenty-eight ways to lose your bully. The chapters are kept short so you can dip in and derive value even if you have only a few minutes to spare. Each chapter ends with an action plan and summary so you can clarify how you're going to put these principles into practice and get real-world results. Discussion questions are provided so you can facilitate group conversations with family members, students, and employees about this challenging and often ignored "elephant in the room" topic.

If you're feeling skeptical, I understand. You may have been stymied by a particularly difficult individual for years, and you're wondering if a book can turn things around. All I can say is that many people have told me these ideas have been life-changing. I hope you'll keep an open mind when reading these pages. Instead of sitting with your mental arms crossed thinking, "That would never work," ask yourself, "How could this work?" Coach Vince Lombardi once said, "Never change a winning game, always change a losing one." If what you've been doing hasn't worked, isn't it worth the effort to give these suggestions a try?

Risky Business?

Retreat, hell! We're just advancing in the opposite direction!
—MARINE GENERAL P. O. SMITH

Please keep this caveat in mind. If your instincts tell you the person you're dealing with is dangerous, take General Smith's advice and advance in the opposite direction. Put your personal safety, rather than your pride, first.

If a crazy driver cuts in front of you on the freeway, let him. So what if you get to your destination ten seconds later? It's not worth giving this person the solitary salute and having him decide to play Destruction Derby with you at 60 miles an hour. I'm not suggesting we turn a blind eye to inappropriate behavior. I'm suggesting we think first before confronting someone who could put us in the hospital (or morgue). As my friend Judy says, "Better smart than sorry."

Hope Is a Risk We Must Run

> Hope is the feeling you have that the feeling you have
> isn't permanent.
> —JEAN KERR

I remember how helpless and hopeless I felt when it looked like unconscionable tactics were going to carry the day. Fortunately, there are specific steps you can take to stop unethical people from trying to take advantage of you—and you don't have to become unethical yourself. If you are ready to find out (1) what constitutes a bully; (2) why bullies behave the way they do; and (3) how you can convince the bully in your life to cease and desist, turn the page and . . . read it and reap. As Alice Walker said, "Human capacity is equal to human cruelty, and it is up to each of us to tip the balance."

28 WAYS TO
LOSE YOUR BULLY

There must be another way,
if only because there has to be.
—HERB CAEN

Way 1. Bully for You?

At the age of four with paper hats and wooden swords
we are all generals—only some of us never grow out of it.
—PETER USTINOV

A WOMAN SAID, "WHEN I THINK OF BULLIES, I PICTURE SOMEONE like Bluto out of the Popeye cartoon. You know, a big brute with hairy arms and bulging biceps. Is that what you're talking about?"

Nope, that's not what we're talking about. Bullies don't necessarily wear black hats or have bulging biceps. They come in all shapes, sizes, genders, ages, and professions. Ninety-year-old grannies can be bullies. Ministers can be bullies. Coaches can be bullies.

A bully is someone who knowingly abuses the rights of others to gain control of the situation and the individual(s) involved. Bullies deliberately and persistently use intimidation and manipulation to get their way. The key words here are *knowingly, deliberately*, and *persistently*.

All of us are difficult on occasion. Bullies are difficult *on purpose*. We may be uncooperative or unpleasant in particular situations. Bullies are uncooperative and unpleasant as part of their

3

strategy. Most of us respond to reasonable efforts to get along. Bullies reject reasonable efforts to get along because they don't want *a* win–win—they want *to* win.

Bullies Aim Below the Belt

> He couldn't see a belt without hitting below it.
> —MARGOT ASQUITH

The following questionnaire can help you determine whether a challenging individual in your life qualifies as a bona fide bully. The question is, does s/he hit below the ethical belt *accidentally* or aim below the ethical belt *intentionally*? If you are dealing with several difficult individuals, take the time to fill this out separately for each one. Answer the questions, rating the frequency of these behaviors from 1 (Rarely) to 3 (Occasionally) to 5 (Often). Go with your instinct. Your first answer is usually the most honest because it comes from the gut, not the intellect.

Bully for You? Questionnaire

	RARELY	OCCASIONALLY		OFTEN
1. Do you "talk on eggshells" around this person and watch everything you say because s/he has a hair-trigger temper?	1 2	3	4	5
2. Does this person act condescending or superior? Does s/he treat you as if you are incompetent?	1 2	3	4	5
3. Is this person hypercritical? Does s/he blame everyone else for what goes wrong?	1 2	3	4	5

4. Does s/he have a Jekyll and Hyde personality? Is s/he charming in public and cruel in private?   1   2   3   4   5

5. Does this person use aggressive body language, inappropriate touching, or physical violence to intimidate you?   1   2   3   4   5

6. Does this person dominate conversations and talk over people who try to get a word in edgewise?   1   2   3   4   5

7. Does this person call you vile names or have derogatory labels for you?   1   2   3   4   5

8. Does this person insist on controlling the decisions (e.g., financial, food, travel) and attack you if you dare question his/her judgment or authority?   1   2   3   4   5

9. Has this person tried to isolate you from friends or family? Is s/he resentful when you spend time with others?   1   2   3   4   5

10. Does this person play martyr and try to make you feel guilty or responsible for his/her moods?   1   2   3   4   5

11. Does this person pick fights or criticize you in public because s/he knows you won't cause a scene?   1   2   3   4   5

12. If you threaten to end the relationship, does this person make nice to get you back and then begin mistreating you again?   1   2   3   4   5

13. If you object to this person's behavior, does s/he go on the offensive and demand to know why *you're* giving her or him such a hard time?   1   2   3   4   5

14. Does this person indulge in crazy-making behavior, such as breaking commitments, reversing statements, or twisting things around and then accusing you of overreacting?   1   2   3   4   5

15. Are you happier when you're *not* around this person?   1   2   3   4   5

Total = _____

35 or below: This individual is *not* a bully. He/she may be unpleasant to deal with once in a while; however, win–win communication on your part will enable the two of you to coexist cooperatively most of the time.

36–55: This person may occasionally exhibit bully behavior. You may need to escalate your response in those situations so s/he understands that that particular behavior is inappropriate. If you keep your cool and communicate constructively, you'll usually be able to resolve what's wrong, repair the relationship, and move forward, not much worse for wear.

56–75: Uh-oh. It looks like you've got a full-blown bully on your hands. Do not pass Go. Do not collect $200. Get your pen out, sit down, and start taking notes so you can begin planning how to stop this individual from running and ruining your life.

No One Deserves to Be Bullied

Chaos, panic, and disorder—my work here is done.
—T-SHIRT SLOGAN

Do you have someone in your life who scores higher than 35 on this test? You're in the right place because we're going to address how to handle every single one of the behaviors mentioned above. We're not going to dwell on how to deal with ordinary difficult people. There are plenty of books that already do a good job of covering that topic. We're going to focus on how to deal with *egregiously* difficult people whose goal is to spread chaos, panic, and disorder.

A woman in a seminar asked, "Why do bullies act the way they do? It's hard for me to understand why anyone would deliberately harm another person." Good question. The next chapter explains what's behind bully behavior. Knowing why they do what they do can keep us from being knocked off balance when they try to pull one of their dirty tricks.

Action Plan and Discussion Questions

Think of the most challenging individual in your life. Does s/he qualify as a bully? Why or why not? _____

_____

_____

_____

Does this individual exhibit other destructive behaviors that weren't on this questionnaire? What are they? _____

_____

_____

_____

Which of these behaviors does s/he indulge in most? Give an example of how s/he does this to you. _____

_____

_____

Now, take the test for yourself. Do you exhibit some of these characteristics? Which ones? _____

_____

_____

If you discovered that *you* sometimes behave like a bully, are you willing to read this book and look for ways you can treat people more compassionately? Explain. _____

_____

_____

Summary

HARMFUL BELIEFS/BEHAVIORS	HELPFUL BELIEFS/BEHAVIORS
Intentionally hurts others *"I'm going to make him sorry he ever met me."*	Occasionally hurts others *"I didn't mean to say that. I'm sorry."*
Rejects reasonable efforts *"It's my way or the highway."*	Responds to reasonable efforts *"Let's figure out what's fair."*
Wants only to win *"If you don't like it, too bad. Take it or leave it."*	Will accept a win–win *"Okay, I'll give a little on this if you agree to that."*
Refuses to admit fault *"You're dead wrong, and I'm not going to listen to you."*	Recognizes when at fault *"I wish that hadn't happened, and I won't do it anymore."*

Runs over others' rights
"I don't give a darn whether your family's upset. This is the way it's going to be."

Respects others' rights
"I don't agree with them on this. However, we'll do it their way when we're in their home."

Aggravates violent individuals
"Hey, you fat jerk, sit down. I can't see the game."

Advances in the opposite direction of violent individuals
"Usher, could you please talk to the man in seat 45B? He's spilling his beer all over everyone."

Way 2. Understand the Nature of the Beast

Were we fully to understand the reasons for other people's behavior,
it would all make sense.
—SIGMUND FREUD

YOU'VE HEARD THE PHRASE "KNOWLEDGE IS POWER"? WELL,
understanding why bullies act the way they do gives us power
because we're not caught off guard by their tactics. If we know
what they're trying to achieve, we can often outwit them
instead of being at wit's end.

People bully for a variety of reasons; the main ones being (1)
they feel inferior and they're compensating; (2) they feel no
remorse; (3) they feel justified; and (4) they lack another way.
Look over the following causes and reflect on which might be
contributing to the destructive disposition of the bullies in
your life. Note that bullies may have one, some, or all of these
triggering factors. Check yes or no by the ones you think
might be motivating your bully to act the way s/he does.

Some People Bully Because They Feel Inferior

The better we feel about ourselves, the fewer times we have to knock someone down in order to feel tall.
—ODETTA

The classic explanation that people bully because they have low self-worth is true much of the time. Look beneath a bully's brusque exterior and you find someone who constantly compares him or herself to other people and comes up short. Bullies hate feeling that others are more talented, popular, or successful. Instead of taking the mature, responsible route to improve themselves so they become better, they take the immature, irresponsible route and make others feel bad so that they can feel better. Many of their aggressive behaviors are designed to prove to the world and themselves that they are superior instead of inferior.

Think about it. Confident people like themselves as they are. They feel no need to put other people down to feel big. Bullies, on the other hand, don't like themselves and compensate for it in a variety of unhealthy ways, including:

- **FAULT-FINDING.** By keeping attention on other people's perceived or projected shortcomings, bullies hope to keep attention off their own. This was humorously pointed out in a classic *Peanuts* cartoon strip. Linus asks Lucy: "Why are you always so anxious to criticize?" Lucy responds, "I just have a knack for seeing other people's faults." Linus protests, "What about your own faults?" Lucy answers, "I have a knack for overlooking them."

  Does the bully in your life pounce on your every mistake? Does s/he focus on your foibles to avoid having to examine or admit her or his own? _____ yes _____ no

- **TAKING CONTROL.** During a *Larry King Live* TV show on CNN, real estate mogul Donald Trump showed his bully stripes. Trump disingenuously asked King, "Do you mind if I sit back a little? Because your breath is very bad. It really is. Has this been told to you before?" King, taken aback, replied, "No." Trump trumped with, "Okay, then, I won't bother."

  Whew! Talk about ambushed! According to producers, Trump was simply showing how to get the edge in negotiations. Right. It appeared that Trump intentionally tried to embarrass his host in front of millions of people so he could get the edge in the interview. Trump didn't want to answer to King; he wanted King to answer to him. He took command of the conversation so he could literally and figuratively run the show.

  Does the bully in your life try to control what you do, who you see, where you go, and how you think? ____ yes ____ no

- **NEEDING TO WIN.** A man named Barry said, "My older brother couldn't stand the thought that I, his younger brother, was a better athlete. He would do anything, anything, to keep me from beating him. If we were playing hoops in our driveway, he would knock me down rather than let me score a winning basket. If we were playing chess, he would sweep the pieces off the board rather than let me checkmate him. One memorable afternoon he threw every single one of his golf clubs into a lagoon when he triple-bogied the seventeenth hole and realized I was going to win our bet." As this little brother found out, bullies resort to whatever tactics are necessary to keep from coming out on the short end.

  Bullies are driven to beat you (or beat you down or beat you up) because they can't bear to be shown up. Winning gives them tangible evidence they're "the best." Does the bully in your life hate to lose because it means you got the best of him or her? Does s/he subscribe to the motto VENI, VIP, VIC ("I came, I'm a very important person, I conquered")? _____ yes _____ no

- **DEFLATING DIGS AND DARK REMARKS.** If you're celebrating something, does the bully in your life try to destroy your good mood with a dark remark? Dark remarks are statements designed to defeat and deflate you. You've heard the saying "Misery loves company"? Bullies don't want you to be lighthearted because they're incapable of feeling that emotion—and they don't want you to experience something they can't. Does the bully in your life hate to see you happy? _____ yes _____ no

  A woman came up to me after a seminar and said, "Now I understand what was going on with my ex-husband. He believed recreational activities were something we should do only when all the chores were done. I disagreed with that and regularly took our kids on excursions to the park, zoo, and pool. We always asked him to join us (sometimes the kids would beg him to come along), but he would always refuse, saying he had work to do. When we would come back into the house laughing and talking about our adventure, he would always do something to wipe the smiles off our faces. He would say something like 'Well, *someone* has to be responsible while you're off gallivanting around town.' In retrospect, I can see that he was deliberately trying to spoil our fun because he was jealous."

- **REFUSING TO APOLOGIZE.** Being a bully means never having to say you're sorry. At least that seems to be the bully philosophy. I had the privilege of meeting Deborah Tannen, author of several groundbreaking books on gender communication including *You Just Don't Understand* and *Talking from 9–5*. Deborah shared a marvelous story about an insight she had had about why some men refuse to apologize or stop to ask for directions. She was watching the scene in the movie *The Kid* in which Bruce Willis's character gets to go back in time and confront the bully who had tormented him throughout his childhood. *This* time, instead of running scared, he stood up to the bully and successfully wrestled him to the ground. What was the one thing he wanted while holding down the bully who had caused him so much humiliation? He demanded, *"Apologize!"*

That moment crystallized Deborah's epiphany that apologizing, for some people, is an issue of dominance and subordination. It means, "I'm wrong, you win!" If you approach things from an adversarial point of view, as bullies do, this turns apologizing into a "one up, one down" interaction. No wonder bullies are reluctant to say they're sorry! They're not about to admit weakness or do anything that puts them at a disadvantage. Does your bully hate to apologize because s/he doesn't want to give you an advantage? _____ yes _____ no

Some People Bully Because They Have an Absence of Remorse

> When are you going to realize that if it doesn't apply to me,
> it doesn't matter?
> —CANDICE BERGEN'S CHARACTER IN THE
> TV SITCOM *MURPHY BROWN*

Remorse is defined as "a gnawing distress arising from a sense of guilt for past wrongs." Guilt is defined as "a feeling of culpability for offenses." Most people who bully feel little or no remorse. This means they don't have any sense of moral obligation that would cause them to examine their behavior, decide it is offensive, and choose to do differently. This lack of culpability means that bullies won't voluntarily change because they don't think about the pain they're causing, they don't *care* about the pain they're causing, or in extreme cases, they *enjoy* the pain they're causing. If you find this notion troubling, rest assured. This book teaches you how to change the way you treat bullies, which can change the way they treat you.

You may be wondering why bullies don't feel remorse. Once again, there are a variety of reasons. Look these over to see which might be behind your bully's inability or refusal to feel empathy or guilt.

- **ARROGANCE.** Gore Vidal said, tongue in cheek (I think), "There is no human problem which could not be solved if people would simply do as I advise." It's ironic that while many bullies feel inferior, some feel they are brilliant beings who are brighter than everyone else. This conceit means they have little tolerance for what they loftily perceive as other people's ineptitude. They have a habit of disdainfully lecturing the "little people" about how things ought to be done because they self-righteously believe they know best about everything. Their motto is: "I'm not rude. You're just insignificant." Does the bully in your life act as if you are beneath him or her? Does s/he treat you with disdain, as if your opinions or wishes don't matter? _____ yes _____ no

- **HAVE "CENTER OF THE UNIVERSE SYNDROME."** A teacher told me, "I have a bully in my class who's all of eight years old. If he sees something he likes, he takes it. If he's told to do something he'd rather not do, he throws a fit. I requested a parent conference, and after five minutes, I knew why Ben was so selfish. His parents, both psychologists, actually told me, 'We don't believe in saying no to Ben. We don't want to stifle his creative freedom.'"

  Yikes. The teacher asked the doting couple, "What if he does something he shouldn't?" They replied calmly, "We divert his attention to something else." No wonder Ben was so ruthless. This wild child was growing up with no boundaries and no rules and no socialization. It never even occurred to him that he needed to consider anyone's feelings but his own.

Does the bully in your life sound like he or she's warming up for a chorus: "Me, me, me, me, me"? Does s/he want it and want it yesterday and woe to you if you get in her or his way? _____ yes _____ no

- **NO NEGATIVE CONSEQUENCES.** A popular Internet joke asks, "If a man is talking in a forest and no women are around, is he still wrong?" Somewhere along the way, bullies misbehaved and no one held them accountable. They concluded, "Well, that may have been wrong, but it worked." At that point, they misbehaved again. If no one objected, they decided the advantages of bullying outweighed the disadvantages—because there *were* no disadvantages. What little regret they may have initially felt was removed because the rewards outweighed the risks.

  You've heard the statement "Let your conscience be your guide"? Since bullies don't have a conscience, they let *consequences* be their guide. If there are no consequences, they have no incentive to change their evil ways.

  You've also heard that "Rewarded behavior gets repeated"? Bully behavior often goes unchallenged, which means it's rewarded, which means it gets repeated. Has your bully gotten off penalty-free? _____ yes _____ no

- **HAVE A CERTIFIABLE PSYCHOLOGICAL OR BIOLOGICAL PROBLEM.** Some bullies have a mental or physical disease that causes them to be unaware of or apathetic about their aberrant behavior. Manic depression, senility, Alzheimer's, and other conditions can cause people to be mean—even when they don't mean to. Character disorders such as antisocial personality disorder can cause sufferers to be dispassionate—devoid of the capacity to feel and act empathetically.

People in pain can also stop caring about anything but their suffering. A nurse told me, "Friendly women can become screaming banshees during labor when push comes to shove. Your world shrinks when you're in agony, and it's almost impossible to think about anything but what hurts. I caution family members not to take it personally if their loved one says or does something hateful because patients are literally and figuratively not themselves."

People can also lose the ability or incentive to judge whether their actions are offensive when they're under the influence of alcohol or drugs. Labels on many over-the-counter and prescription medications warn of dangerous mood swings and heightened irritability. Illegal and controlled substances are disinhibitors, which means the control mechanism in the brain that monitors appropriate behavior is switched off.

Is it possible that your bully is suffering from a mental or physical condition that causes him or her to be unaware that certain behavior is inappropriate? _____ yes _____ no. Is s/he abusing substances? _____ yes _____ no. If yes, see the Resource Directory to find professional assistance to help you deal with this individual safely and effectively.

Some People Bully Because They Feel Justified

> I've been the oppressor and I've been the oppressee. And believe
> me, being the oppressor is better.
> —MAL HANCOCK

Some bullies have convinced themselves they have the right to be mean. Some of their rationalizations include:

- **BEING BROUGHT UP IN A DYSFUNCTIONAL FAMILY.** "When I see the ten most wanted list," Eddie Cantor observed, "I always have this thought that if we'd made them feel wanted earlier, they wouldn't be wanted now." A 1987 University of Finland study researched the origins of violence and concluded that "cruelty or sadism may develop in extreme conditions of rejection and punitiveness. When an individual has been maliciously bullied in his or her developmental years, that individual may retaliate and take pleasure in causing others the pain he/she has suffered." Some bullies grew up in a home where "might was right" and feel that now it's their turn. George V said, "My father was frightened of his mother. I was frightened of my father, and I am damned well going to see to it that my children are frightened of me."

Is the bully in your life a by-product of this Bully Ripple Effect? Is s/he simply doing to others what was done to her or him? _____ yes _____ no

- **ACTING OUT THE THEORY OF DISPLACEMENT.** The theory of displacement states that for some reason, we're afraid to confront or get mad at the person who's causing our pain, so we purge our anger by picking on someone who it's safe to mistreat—someone who's lower on the pecking order. A school counselor told me he sees this played out on his campus every day. As Scott explains, "Maybe the dad got called on the carpet by his boss. He can't tell off his boss, so he comes home and criticizes his wife's cooking. She acts out her resentment by scolding her son for not doing his chores. The son gets back by teasing his little sister about her braces, and she gets even by making fun of the new girl in school." Scott said, "These kids know at some level that what they're doing is wrong, but they can't take it anymore, so they release their tension by taking it out on someone else who's lower on the totem pole."

  Could your bully be afraid to face the real cause of his or her discontent, so he or she is taking it out on you because you're lower in the food chain? _____ yes _____ no

- **CONCLUDING THE BEST DEFENSE IS A GOOD OFFENSE.**
Some people didn't plan on becoming bullies but found themselves in a "survival of the meanest" environment where they felt they had to be bullies to survive. A woman contractor said, "As the only woman in a male-dominated industry, my partner was constantly being tested. Every day she faced an 'if you're not part of the steamroller, you're part of the road' situation. She finally resorted to being aggressive so she could hold her own with the macho construction guys. The problem is, now she can't turn it off." Has the bully in your life adopted a "demeanor da better" approach? _____ yes _____ no

Some People Bully Because They Lack Another Way

> I don't think we have to teach people how to be human.
> I think we have to teach them how not to be inhuman.
> —ELDRIDGE CLEAVER

Actually, I think we do need to teach people how to communicate with others so they're not inhuman. If bullying is all someone has experienced, he or she may lack the ability to do it differently. If role models did not exhibit or teach them people skills, bullies may simply not know how to "play well with others." Unfortunately, having rough edges becomes a type of double jeopardy for bullies. Since they have so much invested in a gruff style that renders them reluctant to admit any failing, they will often continue to be a bully rather than humble themselves to seek help or admit they need assistance. Maintaining the status quo seems easier than getting out of their comfort zone.

A walking buddy of mine told me about a member of the board of their community association who fit this description perfectly. Karen said, "This woman loves to stir things up."

Karen corrected herself: "Forget that, she *lives* to stir things up. She seems to operate on the belief that negative attention is better than no attention. This woman finds things to fuss about. If we don't have a contentious issue to handle, she'll create one just to prolong the meetings and be in the middle of things.

"I've come to the conclusion that she's lonely and her life is rather empty. Her involvement on this committee is probably the only thing she has to look forward to. The problem is, she doesn't know how to relate to people. I think she says outrageous things just to engage people so she doesn't get ignored. The irony is, she feels everyone is against her. Well, everyone *is* against her because her nitpicky style is so off-putting. The sad part is, she ends up being even more isolated because people go out of their way to avoid her. She would never in a million years think of herself as a bully, and she would never for a minute realize she's the source of her own problem."

Sound familiar? Do the bullies in your life alienate people because of their lack of social skills? Do they feel like the victim even though they're the ones behaving objectionably? Does their perception that they're being persecuted become a self-fulfilling prophecy because they're antagonizing people with their gracelessness? _____ yes _____ no

What's Behind Your Bully?

Some people cling to pains, real and imagined, to excuse what they have become.
—LILLIAN HELLMAN

Did you get some "Aha's!" about what might be behind your bully's motives and actions? The good news is, when you know what he or she's trying to do and why, you can often defeat his or her purpose.

A wise day-care worker provided an excellent example of how understanding a bully's motivation can help us nip inappropriate behavior in the bud. Julie always seemed to know just what to do when dealing with children who were, shall we say, a bit on the spoiled side. One day a new parent brought her rambunctious son into the preschool for the first time. While the mother filled out the required paperwork, her son spied a plastic baseball bat in the toy bin. He marched over, picked it up, took a few swings, then started whacking kids with it. Julie quietly walked over, took it from him, said "No!" firmly, and locked the bat in the closet.

The child promptly threw himself on the ground and started wailing as if he had just lost his best friend (which he obviously had). His embarrassed mother bustled over and asked Julie to please give the bat back to her son. She explained that he "didn't mean to hit the other children"; it was just that he was "too young to know that what he was doing was wrong."

Julie looked at the mother calmly and said simply, *"He knows now."*

Bravo. Julie had just nipped in the bud a bully in the making. Up until that child met his match, he was learning that if you don't get your way, all you have to do is make a big fuss and people will give in to you. Thankfully for everyone who would be dealing with this little bruiser, Julie introduced him to the world of consequences. She was not vulnerable to his manipulation because she saw it for what it was. Most important, she was not about to excuse it because she knew where such behavior would lead if it wasn't stopped now.

This example brings up the point that some of us are unknowingly contributing to a bully's misbehavior. The next chapter helps you examine your beliefs to see if they're helping or hurting you. You may discover, like this child's mother did, that idealistic naïveté may be unwittingly adding fuel to the bully's fire.

Action Plan and Discussion Questions

Did you get any "Aha's" that help you understand why people become bullies? What are they? _____

_____

_____

_____

What are two factors behind your bully's behavior? Explain why you think they motivate this person to misbehave or mistreat others. _____

_____

_____

_____

Did you recognize any of these factors as part of your personality? Which of these characteristics do you relate to and why? _____

_____

_____

_____

Do you feel different about the bully in your life now that you know why he/she may act that way? Explain. _____

_____

_____

_____

Summary

HARMFUL BELIEFS/BEHAVIORS	HELPFUL BELIEFS/BEHAVIORS
Feels inferior, so belittles others to feel big *"This is full of mistakes. You really messed this up."*	Feels secure, so no need to prove self *"Let's talk about how this could be improved."*
Compulsive need to control *"I'll take care of this. If it's going to get done right, I have to handle it."*	Likes to share control *"If we divvy this up, we can get it finished today."*
Burning desire to win *"I don't know why they put you in charge. You're not up to the task."*	Seeks a win-win *"Together we can do a quality job."*
Arrogant—convinced has no faults *"Why am I the only one who can be counted on to do things right?"*	Confident—admits faults *"It was my fault that I didn't clarify those instructions."*
Absence of remorse *"Nobody ever cared about me, so why should I care about them?"*	Takes responsibility *"I'm going to apologize for making a joke at her expense."*
No negative consequences and no conscience *"These people just let anyone push them around. What wimps."*	Holds self and others accountable and answers to conscience *"Taking my anger out at you was uncalled for. I'm sorry."*

Feels bully behavior is justified
"I'm tired of being jerked around. She's going to pay for this."

Feels assertive behavior is right
"I'm going to speak up and let her know this is unacceptable."

Lacks another way
"Get out of my way. I hate you!"

Learns another way
"I'm going to sign up for that people skills class."

Way 3. Update Idealistic Expectations

The significant problems we face cannot be solved at the same level of thinking with which they were created.
—ALBERT EINSTEIN

SIMPLY PUT, WE CAN'T RESPOND TO BULLIES THE WAY WE HAVE IN the past, or we'll reap the same unsatisfactory results. The problem is, many of us have idealistic ideas about how people ought to act. These "wishful thinking" beliefs undermine our effectiveness because we're emotionally knocked out every time people behave in ways we think they shouldn't.

This chapter identifies several convictions that make matters worse, and recommends replacements that can contribute to, rather than compromise, our bully-busting efforts. Ask if your ingrained opinions about how people are supposed to act could be undermining your ability to neutralize the intimidating individuals in your life.

Turn Harmful Expectations into Helpful Epiphanies

> Expectations are resentments under construction.
> —ANNE LAMOTT

Epiphanies are sudden, mind-opening revelations that allow us to perceive a subject in a more realistic, personally meaningful way. Adopting the following "insight information" can support your quest to not let people take advantage of you.

Idealistic Expectation: If I'm Nice to People, They'll Be Nice to Me
Realistic Epiphany: The Nicer We Are to Bullies, the Meaner They'll Be to Us

> Kind words soothe and quiet and comfort the hearer. They shame him out of his sour, morose, unkind feelings. We have not yet begun to use kind words in such abundance as they ought to be used.
> —BLAISE PASCAL

Au contraire. While Pascal's observation is true in most cases, many interviewees told me they've already used an abundance of kind words with the sour person in their life—to no avail.

Webster's defines a bully as someone who is habitually cruel to others weaker than himself. Bullies don't pick on powerful people, they pick on people who won't fight back. For a bully, that translates into a nice person. Bullies *love* nice people because nice people can be counted on to continue being kind even when they're being treated cruelly.

A psychologist friend once told me that "Our strength taken to an extreme becomes our weakness." As Diane explained, "A social person who loves being with people, taken to an extreme, develops into someone who can't abide being alone.

A funny person with an ability to make people laugh, taken to an extreme, can become a manic personality who always has to be on."

Kindness, taken to an extreme, becomes our emotional Achilles' heel. As William Blake said, "He has observed the Golden Rule, Till he's become the Golden Fool." When we are dealing with someone whose goal is to control, ethical approaches can invite exploitation because they're construed as softness. While we're seeking mutuality, bullies are seeking dominance.

It can be disillusioning to discover that one of our best qualities has worked against us. Rest assured, you'll learn exactly what to do if someone is abusing your good nature in Way 11, "Police Your Puh-lease." For now, simply ask yourself if your benevolence has backfired with the bully in your life.

Idealistic Expectation: Silence Is Golden
Realistic Epiphany: Silence Emboldens Bullies

> I never regretted a single thing I didn't say.
> —CALVIN COOLIDGE

Coolidge's quote, along with many others about the advantage of holding our tongue, are all-or-nothing generalizations. They make the across-the-board recommendation that "no response is often the best response."

It's true that refraining from spouting off in the heat of the moment can help us respond wisely instead of rashly. Tongue Glue (biting our tongue instead of letting loose what's on the tip of our tongue) can keep us from saying something we regret.

Unfortunately, when we turn the other cheek with a bully, they'll slap that one, too. Remember, bullies are not going to reflect on their actions and realize the error of their ways. They won't admonish themselves with "This person doesn't deserve this. I'm going to apologize." No, bullies think, "Great! I mis-treated this person and he or she didn't protest. I'll interpret that as a green light."

From now on, realize that silence sanctions. As you'll dis-cover in Way 6, "Get Out of My Space," bullies will continue to invade our emotional turf unless we establish and enforce verbal boundaries. You may be thinking, "But my mind goes blank and I get tongue-tied when someone's mean to me. That's why I don't speak up." You'll learn exactly what to say when you don't know what to say—in Way 9, "Beat 'Em to the Punch . . . Line."

Idealistic Expectation: Active Listening Promotes Understanding
Realistic Epiphany: Active Listening Perpetuates Abuse

> One of the best ways to persuade others is with
> your ears—by listening to them.
> —DEAN RUSK

Rusk is right in that perceiving things from the other person's perspective is an important ingredient of persuasive communi-cation. It works though only if the other person is equally interested in reaching a mutual understanding.

Giving bullies empathetic attention gives them an unde-served "bully pulpit." Continuing to give them our compas-sionate attention grants them unwarranted carte blanche opportunities to dominate our mind and time.

Dr. Jacob Azerrad, author of *Anyone Can Have a Happy Child,* believes Americans attend more to bad behavior than to good behavior. He believes this is due to "kiddie gurus who repeatedly urge parents to soothe, comfort, and talk to a child who screams, throws things, or otherwise acts in obnoxious, infantile ways." He points out that the more faithfully parents follow this foolish advice, the worse their children behave. Azerrad suggests that "Instead of playing therapist, parents need to teach their children how to calmly handle things that don't go their way."

Agreed. It's time to stop playing therapist to *adult* bullies who throw tantrums when they don't get their way. We need to stop giving them a willing, sympathetic audience and start teaching them they can't get away with obnoxious, infantile behavior. Way 15, "Put All Kidding Aside," teaches you how to cut bullies off in mid-sentence so they can no longer bend your ear or will—at will.

Idealistic Expectation: Crying Purges Emotions
Realistic Epiphany: Crying Produces More Emotion

> Grief is the agony of an instant; the indulgence of
> grief the blunder of a life.
> —BENJAMIN DISRAELI

One of the biggest lessons I've learned about dealing with bullies is that, past a point, crying makes us meek and keeps us weak. For months I was in a state of shock as the bully I was dealing with broke commitments and disobeyed court orders, and the authorities did nothing to hold this person accountable. The constant barrage of character assassination designed to break my spirit almost did just that. I wore out the phone talking to a few close friends looking for advice, solace, and (I now realize) sympathy.

In essence, I was feeling sorry for myself. Although my despair was justified, my sister, bless her heart, finally told me that my "Poor me" and "Ain't it awful" attitudes were perpetuating the problem. She was right. Self-pity preserves the bully-victim loop.

Tears have been called the safety valve of the heart and summer showers to the soul. Crying can be a healthy, tangible way to purge grief. Pouring out the tidal wave of frustration to a trusted friend or therapist can help us survive and arrive at our "dark night of the soul-ution."

However, as Voltaire said, "The longer we dwell on our misfortunes, the greater is their power to harm us." In other words, weeping keeps us wounded. There comes a time when it is to our advantage to stop crying and start trying. Once we have mourned and allowed ourselves to feel the sadness that accompanies being bullied, it's time to regain our strength and self-respect. One way to do that is to stop complaining about the situation and start planning what we're going to do about it. Way 5, "Become a Verbal Samurai" shows you how to do just that.

Idealistic Expectation: Wrongdoers Are Responsible for Fixing the Problem
Realistic Epiphany: The Person Being Wronged Is Responsible for Fixing the Problem

People treat you the way you teach them to treat you.
—JACK CANFIELD

We need to accept that even if what's happening isn't our fault, it is our responsibility. This may seem grossly unfair. It is also the way it is, and the sooner we learn this lesson, the better off we'll be.

Why is this so important? Because, as an anonymous philosopher once said, "There are no victims without volunteers." You may protest, "I don't agree with this. Innocent children who are abused didn't volunteer for that." You are absolutely right in pointing out that innocent children are not responsible for being mistreated.

There are also adult exemptions. A man in a seminar objected, "I'm a victim of a drunk driver, and the idea that I somehow created this offends me. I was sitting at a traffic light waiting for the light to turn green when this guy who was ten sheets to the wind plowed into the back of my car. I was in a hospital for three weeks, and I've spent the last ten months in physical therapy. My car was totaled; the driver didn't have insurance; and I've spent hours on the phone trying to take care of bills that I shouldn't even have had to pay in the first place. You can't tell me that I somehow asked for all the misery this guy has put me through."

This is an important distinction. I am not suggesting we bring bullies into our life, and I am not saying we're to blame for what's happened. I am saying we are responsible for fixing what's happened. While we may not have provoked these unfortunate circumstances, we can't expect bullies to come to their senses and make amends . . . because they won't.

Sally Kempton said, "It's hard to fight an enemy who has an outpost in your head." Waiting for wrongdoers to do right by us means our peace of mind is in their hands. This incident and individual may be out of sight, but they are not out of mind. For our own mental health, we need to move on, and the way to move on, even if we're still in the midst of an ugly situation, is to see it as our trial by fire.

At some point in our lives, all of us have probably had some cross to bear. We have suffered, or will suffer, a disaster or an injustice. At that point, as fellow speaker W. Mitchell says, "We have a choice. We either focus on what we can no longer do or on what we can do."

Mitchell ought to know. Riding his motorcycle through the streets of San Francisco, he was blindsided by a laundry truck. The resulting crash and fire left him with no fingers and a disfigured face. Being the original eternal optimist, Mitchell recovered from those injuries and continued on with his life—

becoming the mayor of Crested Butte, Colorado, and running for congress.

Then, while taking off from a small airport, the private plane Mitchell was piloting lost power and crashed. After helping his passengers to safety, Mitchell found he couldn't get out of the plane. He was paralyzed from the waist down.

For many people, two life-shattering incidents in the span of a few years would have been the proverbial last straw; they would have descended into despair. Not Mitchell. At last count, he has traveled to more than thirty countries and spoken to more than half a million people in his mission to share his inspiring message that it's not what happens to you, it's what you do about it.

As Mitchell knows from experience, as I now know, and as you have already learned or will learn, when life (or a bully) knocks us down, we can stay down, feeling sorry for ourselves, lamenting all the while how unfair this is, or we can get up, brush ourselves off, extract insight, and move on. As Ernest Hemingway said, "The world breaks everyone, and afterward many are strong at the broken places."

Bullying Is a Test of Your Self-Respect

> People always say I didn't give up my seat because I was tired, but that isn't true. No, the only tired I was, was tired of giving in.
> —ROSA PARKS

Are you tired of giving in to a bully who has been undermining your self-respect and quality of life? Do you understand that how you respond to a bully defines and shapes who you are and how you perceive yourself? Resolve to adopt thought processes that support rather than sabotage your ability to stand up for yourself.

You've probably heard Edmund Burke's famous quote that

"The only thing necessary for the triumph of evil is for good men to do nothing." Understand that if you do nothing, bullies will continue to perpetrate their evil on you. The next chapter demonstrates that once we vow to stop being a victim, we can start rectifying unsatisfactory situations by staging a conflict resolution evolution.

Action Plan and Discussion Questions

Did you recognize any of these outdated expectations as ones that you have? Which ones? _____

_____

_____

_____

How have these outmoded beliefs compromised your effectiveness in neutralizing a negative individual's impact? _____

_____

_____

Do you have any additional epiphanies that can help you transcend unfortunate or unfair circumstances? What are they? _____

_____

_____

Has your kindness or silence made the situation better or worse? Explain. _____

_____

_____

_____

Have you "cried buckets," as one lady confessed? How has it helped? How has it hurt? Is it time to dry your tears? Why or why not? _____

_____

_____

Could it help to see this as your trial by fire? How so? _____

_____

_____

Do you agree with the idea that "There are no victims without volunteers"? Why or why not? _____

_____

_____

Do you see yourself as a victim? If so, what benefits do you derive from considering yourself a victim? _____

_____

_____

Do you agree that it's your responsibility to fix the problem, even if the bully is to blame? Why or why not? _____

_____

_____

Summary

HARMFUL BELIEFS/BEHAVIORS	HELPFUL BELIEFS/BEHAVIORS
Have outdated expectations *"This is the third time they've come home an hour late and not apologized or paid me extra."*	Have updated epiphanies *"They must think they're getting away with this, and they're hoping I don't bring it up."*
Be kind to others and they'll be kind to you *"If I do a really good job, surely they'll notice and reward me."*	Understand that kindness can become our weakness *"I can't count on them taking the initiative on this."*
Silence is golden *"Well, I don't want to seem forward. I'll keep quiet and they'll pay me next time."*	Silence emboldens bullies *"Mr. and Mrs. Jones, could you please pay for the extra hour I stayed tonight?"*
Crying purges emotions *"I'm so hurt that they'd take advantage of me like this."*	Weep no more *"Okay, enough of that. Crying won't change things."*
Wait for wrongdoers to fix things *"They should keep track of this."*	Take responsibility for fixing things *"Mr. and Mrs. Jones, I've printed up a bill with tonight's charges."*

Way 4. Stage a Conflict Resolution Evolution

Some people can be reasoned into sense, and others
must be shocked into it.
—THOMAS PAINE

ONE WOMAN SAID, "I'VE TRIED EVERYTHING I'VE KNOWN TO DO
to get this person to leave me alone, and she's still bothering
me." I told her it's probably because she used three of the four
"AAAApproaches to Dealing with Bullies" that *don't* work.

AVOID: Many people think that staying out of a bully's way will
prevent or solve the problem. Wrong. What they're not taking
into account is that bullies pursue their targets. Once a bully
has fixated on you, trying to steer clear is completely ineffective because the bully will find you. He or she will seek you
out even if you're doing everything you can to stay out of the
crosshairs.

ACCOMMODATE: People who hate ugliness often end up making unhealthy compromises to prevent confrontations. The
problem is, bullies know this and purposely play it to their advantage. Accommodating bullies perpetuates their intimidation
because they know people will back down in the face of their

aggression. People who go along to get along better learn how to get along without their self-respect, because they won't have much.

ASSERT: As you'll discover later in this chapter, asserting ourselves in the traditional sense doesn't dissuade bullies, it delights them. Telling a bully "I don't like what you're doing" is exactly what s/he wants to hear. The whole point is for us to be bothered by their behavior.

Are you wondering, "If these three approaches don't work, what does?" The answer may surprise you.

The Fourth AAAApproach to Dealing with Bullies—Aggression

> If you feel like you're a second-class citizen, you are.
> —TED TURNER

If you're being treated like a second-class citizen, you might want to consider the advice of a school psychologist who offered the following opinion during a public seminar. We were discussing the "price of nice" when this woman chuckled and said, "I've worked in schools for more than thirty years. One of the most important lessons I've learned is that sometimes you've got to bully the bully to get his attention and respect."

You might be thinking, "Did I read this right? Did the author really just suggest we become bullies ourselves?!" As you'll discover in this book, I'm not suggesting you become a bully. I am suggesting that out-bullying bullies is sometimes the *only* thing that will convince them to cut it out. Ironically, the only people bullies admire (and leave alone) are the ones who don't let them get away with their brutish behavior.

Can We Have a Show of Strength?

My greatest strength is that I have no weakness.
—JOHN McENROE

Responding with a show of strength is not abandoning our
ethics; it is understanding that we can't solve our bully problem
by responding with the same pacifist behavior that prompted
them to pick on us in the first place. "Shocking some sense
into them" is sometimes what's required to stop bullies in their
verbal tracks. When it is clear that we will not tolerate abuse,
we reverse the risk-reward ratio and they will often choose to
leave us alone.

This "bully the bully" conclusion was reached after much
soul-searching and philosophical torment. In fact, I delayed
writing this book for months because I didn't want readers to
misinterpret my message and think I was advocating that we
become more combative. Please note that I am not suggesting
we abandon our commitment to being kind. I believe kindness
is a moral and practical choice, and most of the time we'll be
glad that we've chosen to treat others with the courtesy they
want, need, and deserve.

At the same time, we need to understand that unethical people will try to take advantage of our compassion. Collaborative
communication will continue to be our preferred approach—
provided the people we're dealing with care about being fair! If
they're not, all bets are off. After interviewing hundreds of people who've successfully dealt with bullies, and after reflecting
on my own experience, I've concluded that "It is right to be
strong when someone is (persistently) in the wrong."

In fact, not only is aggression occasionally appropriate, it is
sometimes exactly what the situation requires.

Suit Yourself

I believe in benevolent dictatorships, provided I am the dictator.
—RICHARD BRANSON, BRITISH ENTREPRENEUR

Let me explain. During the last fifty years, the thought about which leadership style works best has changed. Several decades ago, autocratic leadership was the norm. Autocratic leadership means, "I'm the boss, I tell you what to do; you do it. I give orders, you follow them."

Then, in a move prompted by Edward Deming, Peter Drucker, and other respected management gurus, participative leadership became the preferred style. Participative leadership theory says, "It's better to ask employees for their opinion and include them in decision-making so they 'own' the process." This movement spawned quality circles, in which workers contributed their suggestions so they felt involved and appreciated.

Next, it was decided that neither style is right or wrong. Industry experts suggested that situational leadership, suiting your management style to the specific workplace profile, is best. For example, it is better to be an autocratic leader with new hires. It is silly to ask new employees for their opinions when they don't have any job experience. It's better to give clear directions so these new workers know exactly what's expected of them.

Likewise, it's wise to be more of a participative manager with long-time staff members. It's an insult to their intelligence and expertise to order them around. It's smart to invite their valuable input so they feel honored and so the organization can capitalize on workers' insights gained from their front-line experience.

One Conflict Resolution Style Does Not Fit All

> When I first went into the active army, you could tell someone to move a chair across the room—now you have to tell him why.
> —MAJOR ROBERT LEMKE

I believe we need to go through a similar progression of recommended conflict resolution styles. Several decades ago, the most popular self-help books proposed that we look out for number one. The common wisdom was to get smart about negotiating techniques so that we could get the best possible deal for ourselves. We were in the middle of the cold war and the emphasis was on "the best defense is a good offense."

Then came the advent of win-win. It was proposed that cooperative approaches were the right and only way to reach enduring resolutions. Even in foreign policy, the tone was conciliatory, with "peace with honor" the desired goal.

Why Win-Win Doesn't Work with a Jerk

> It is not enough to succeed. Others must fail.
> —GORE VIDAL

They don't call this man Gore for nothing. Unfortunately, many of us have found out the hard way that fair-minded approaches fizzle when dealing with individuals who want not just to succeed, but to have us fail. An attorney friend puts it this way: "Getting into a negotiation with a bully and hoping he'll be ethical because you're being ethical . . . is like getting into a ring with a bull and hoping he won't charge because you're a vegetarian."

That's why it's in our best interests to adopt a situational conflict resolution style. Just as neither the autocratic or participative leadership approach is necessarily good or bad, neither the "number one" or the "win-win" approach is necessarily good or bad. Just as we came to understand that it's wise to match our management style to the employee we're working with, it's wise to adapt our communication style to the individual we're dealing with.

We'll continue to relate in win-win ways with most people, because most people are reasonable beings who want to coexist cooperatively. However, if we're dealing with those who have a history of sweeping aside our sincere efforts to get along, it is appropriate and even advisable to cut them off so they no longer get a free deride at our expense.

Bullies Use Words as Weapons

> You can stroke people with words.
> —F. SCOTT FITZGERALD

Anyone who's dealt with a bully knows that bullies strike people with words. A woman in a seminar said she'd gone to high school with a gossip queen who was one of those "if I never see her again, it'll be too soon" types. Monica said, "Every girl in our school was afraid of her because you never knew what was going to come out of her mouth. She'd give you these backhanded compliments like 'You should wear stripes more often. They're very slenderizing.' Or 'Did you get a haircut? Your face looks thinner.' I knew I was going to run into her at our high school's tenth reunion and I was determined not to let her ruin my evening. Sure enough, she started walking across the dance floor with that spiteful gleam in her eye as soon as she saw me. Before she could say a word, I put my hand up and said, 'Beth, don't even start' and turned and walked away."

Don't Be Afraid to Be Forceful

> I can't understand why people are afraid of new ideas. I'm
> frightened of the old ones.
> —JOHN CAGE

This type of "don't even think about parking here" response has not been considered a viable option by many relationship experts, and I feel many of us have suffered as a result. A woman named Sheila who attended one of my workshops said, "I can't tell you what a relief it is to hear this. I bought into the idea that 'win-win' was the only option, so I felt like a failure when it failed to work. I thought somehow I just hadn't tried hard enough or long enough or been smart enough to pull it off. After years of putting up with a verbally abusive husband, I finally summoned the courage to complain to my mother, and she told me it was the woman's duty to make her marriage work and I should try harder to be a good wife. I confided in a friend who was in a Twelve Step program and she told me to 'stop taking his inventory.' Self-help books kept telling me that 'love would conquer all' and that I should adopt Gandhi's philosophy and 'be the change I wished to see.' My therapist must have been a fan of *The Total Woman* (you know, the book that suggested we meet our husband at the door wrapped in Saran Wrap?) because she kept telling me I needed to be 'more supportive of my mate.'"

She shook her head in exasperation at those frustrating years. "Being supportive was what got me in trouble in the first place. The nicer I was to him, the nastier he was to me. I wish someone had told me back then that standing up to him would have worked better than sympathizing with him."

Might Is Not Right—Don't Join the Bully Club

> I've got a good mind to join a club and beat
> you over the head with it.
> —GROUCHO MARX IN *DUCK SOUP*

Point of clarification. A show of force does not mean retaliating, which is defined as "exacting revenge, repaying in kind." Revenge is not our goal. Our goal is simply to behave forcefully in ways that dissuade bullies from attacking us now and in the future. Aggression is not our first option, it's our last resort. We don't want to allow ourselves to be victimized; neither are we going to victimize others. In other words, no joining Groucho's club and beating people over the head. Only when people refuse to respond to peaceful efforts to coexist do we escalate our behavior in order to equalize the balance of power. You're probably wondering, "But how do we escalate our behavior without becoming a bully ourselves?" The answer is to become a Verbal Samurai.

Action Plan and Discussion Questions

Do you agree that it's appropriate to suit your conflict resolution style to the situation? Why or why not? _____
_____
_____

What is your standard approach to dealing with difficult people? Do you avoid, accommodate, assert, or go on the aggressive? Give an example. _____
_____
_____

Think of an unfair situation you're dealing with right now. Do you think it's time to have a show of force to reverse the risk-reward ratio? How so? _____

_____

_____

Summary

HARMFUL BELIEFS/BEHAVIORS	HELPFUL BELIEFS/BEHAVIORS
Respond to bullies by avoiding, accommodating, or asserting *"Oh, no, here comes Ned. Let me duck into this hallway."*	Respond to bullies with conflict resolution style appropriate to situation *"Ned, don't even start with me."*
Pacifist who avoids confrontation *"Come on, what did I do to you?"*	Strategist who understands it's sometimes advisable to be strong *"Here, let me get my pen. Do you want to repeat that for the record?"*
Win-win approach all the time *"Can't we just get along?"*	Win-win when people play fair *"One more word and you'll force me to report you."*
Might is right *"I'm going to haul off and sock him one."*	Might for right *"Put a sock in it or this is going in your personnel file."*

Way 5. Become a Verbal Samurai

The need for change bulldozed a road down
the center of my mind.
—MAYA ANGELOU

IF SOMEONE HAS BEEN BULLDOZING A DESTRUCTIVE PATH DOWN
the center of your life, it's time to change his or her evil ways
by learning how to be a Verbal Samurai.

Samurais were highly trained sword fighters in Japan in the
1600s; they served and protected their masters. These warriors
did not go out looking for fights; however, if someone was
foolish enough to pick a fight with them, the samurais would
use their superior strength and skill to emerge victorious.
Opponents were hesitant to challenge them, because they
knew in advance they stood little chance of winning.

When a samurai's master died, he was sometimes set free to
"do ronin," to embark upon a spiritual quest for personal
development. Some samurai found it difficult to operate
autonomously because they were so accustomed to answering
to someone higher than themselves. Over time they learned to
become their own master and achieved the distinction of
becoming a ronin samurai.

Do you see the parallel? You may have become accustomed
to answering to someone more *contentious* than yourself. Our
goal, like that of a ronin samurai, is to become autonomous
instead of allowing others to lord over us.

A Verbal Samurai in Action

A man does what he must—in spite of obstacles, dangers, and
pressures—and that is the basis of all human morality.
—JOHN F. KENNEDY

Verbal Samurais (both male and female) do what they must to
prevent people from unfairly pressuring them and/or putting
them in psychological or physical danger.

A friend's daughter provided a role model of what it means
to be a Verbal Samurai. This confident young woman was graduating from Georgetown University the same week her sister
was graduating from high school in Hawaii. Her single mom
couldn't be in both places at once and had elected to attend the
ceremony on Maui. What none of them anticipated was the
ex-husband (who was "father non grata") showing up unin-
vited at the older daughter's graduation.

True to form, the hypercritical father approached his daughter moments after she had received her diploma and started in:
"You just wasted four years of your life. Why'd you get a
degree in political science, anyway? You're never going to be
able to find a job. You just threw away thousands of dollars."

He would have continued his verbal assault, but the self-
assured young woman put her hand up and startled her father
into silence. She looked him in the eye and said slowly and
forcefully, "Dad, *stop.* Do I look like my mother?"

His mouth dropped open. She continued, "I'm proud of
myself for graduating from this university, and I'm glad I got

this degree. If you are here to help me celebrate, you're welcome to stay. If you're not, leave."

Bravo. That was samurai behavior. She took command of the situation and did what was necessary to stop the attack. She didn't lose control and start calling her father names. She didn't wilt under his mean-spirited remarks and break into tears. She didn't cry, "Why are you doing this to me?" She didn't passively endure his inappropriate behavior, only to go home later, devastated that he had ruined her big day. In no uncertain terms, she let her dad know his behavior was unacceptable and would not be tolerated. She spoke up instead of suffering in silence and held him accountable for his hurtful words. She also posed a constructive option that gave him a face-saving out.

Like this savvy young woman, we don't want to be a wimp and we don't want to go on the warpath. We want to have the strength and skills to speak up on our own behalf, instead of passively allowing others to master us.

Yes, I Do Mind!

> It's the worst thing that can happen. People will come saying,
> "Bear up—trust to time." No, they're wrong. Mind it.
> —E. M. FORSTER

Sometimes, people bear bully behavior because they're passively hoping that time will wound all heels (oops, I mean heal all wounds!). If they're insulted, they brush it off and think, "I don't mind." If someone mistreats them, they think, "It doesn't matter." It does matter, and you should mind.

Bullies count on us being afraid of them. Their modus operandi is to manipulate you into a moral cul-de-sac where *you're* forced to be the "bad guy." Since you don't want to be the bad guy, you end up tolerating situations you would never endure otherwise.

This was what was happening to a woman who consulted with me. She was a single mom of six adult children. Her one daughter had married an extremely possessive man who had emotionally blackmailed her into breaking off contact with her family. When they did show up at holiday gatherings he would ruin the occasion by barking orders at his wife, interrupting people right and left, and offending everyone at the table with bigoted, racist opinions. This woman was heartsick about what was happening to her daughter, but felt helpless. Her daughter had been so coopted, she wouldn't listen to warnings.

The family had put up with this man's antisocial behavior because they wanted to maintain contact with their daughter and sister, even if it was just a couple of times a year. The mother confided, "We've come up with a plan. This Thanksgiving, if he starts in on one of his tirades, we're all going to get up and leave the table. That ought to teach him."

Who's Teaching Whom What Lesson?

> If you don't run your own life, somebody else will.
> —JOHN ATKINSON

I looked at her, dismayed. She asked, "You don't think that's a good idea?" I said, "This analogy might give you an insight into what's happening. A young couple bought their first apartment and filled it with brand new furniture. The next weekend they went to the animal shelter and got a cat. The cat had been in its new home for only a few minutes when it started sharpening its claws on the sofa. The wife rushed over, picked up the cat, and put it outside. Later in the day the cat started kneading the sofa again with its claws. The husband rushed over, picked it up, and put it outside. So from then on, whenever the cat wanted to go outside . . ."

I told the woman, "We have to ask ourselves, 'Who's teaching who what lesson?' This couple wasn't training the cat, the cat was training them. Abandoning your holiday meal won't teach your son-in-law the lesson you want. He's training *you* to continue to accommodate his abominable behavior. Think of the power you give him by getting up and leaving your own table in your own home.

"I know you feel he's got you over a barrel because you don't want to lose your daughter. The point is, he's holding everyone hostage. It's time for *him* to pay the consequences for his behavior instead of everyone else. When dealing with bullies, we need to honor the majority. Instead of *many* people sacrificing their rights to honor one individual's misbehavior, the one individual needs to change his or her behavior to honor the group's rights."

Don't Let Bullies Hold You Hostage

If you put a small value on yourself, rest assured that the world will not raise your price.
—Anonymous

The woman asked, "What should we do?" I suggested, "Act as the matriarch and take charge. Tell your daughter your plans first so she's prepared, and then take him aside alone *before* everyone sits down. Tell him, 'Things are going to be different from now on. We value family, and our holiday meals are going to be a celebration of that. That means you will treat my daughter and everyone else in our home with respect. That means you will not share hateful, bigoted opinions at the table. That means you'll listen to what other people have to say without interrupting. This is our home and these are our rules. If you want to join us, you need to abide by them. If you choose not to honor these rules, you will be asked to leave and our daughter will stay. This is not open to discussion or second chances, so don't test us on this.' "

I told the woman, "Then walk away. *Don't* engage him in conversation. You are laying down the law; this is not open to debate. Don't ask if he agrees with this. It doesn't matter if he likes it, what matters is that the family's values are being honored. Don't let him put you on the defensive. You are not being heartless, you are simply holding him accountable for decent behavior.

"If he acts up at the table, stand, point to the door, and say, 'Roger, get your things and go.' If he turns to his wife and blusters, 'You're coming with me,' increase the *intensity* of your voice, look him in the eye, and say distinctly, 'Don't you *dare* put her in the middle of this. Margaret is staying here and finishing her dinner. You knew the rules. Now, leave.' "

Now Is Not the Time to Be Timid

You have got to have courage. I don't care how good a man is,
if he is timid, his value is limited. The timid will not amount to
much in this world. I want to see a good man able to hold
his own in active life against the force of evil.
—THEODORE ROOSEVELT

I shared this story with a workshop audience. A concerned mother spoke up and said, "What if that son-in-law browbeat his wife into leaving with him anyway, and he cut off all communication with the family?"

I said, "You're right, there is a risk of that, and it would be unfortunate. It's important to understand, though, that the son-in-law is using the family's fear as a way of coercing them to put up with his offensive behavior. This is what bullies do; they make everyone else pay while they get their way. They create double-bind situations where your only options are lose-lose.

"If that happened, I hope the family reminds themselves that they didn't ask for or want this unfortunate situation. The bully has perpetrated it upon them and it's up to them to put a halt to his emotional tyranny. The alternative of continuing to tip-toe around his tantrums serves no one.

"In the final analysis, I still think it's better to call him on his behavior because if the family doesn't stand up to him, the daughter never will. Refusing to indulge his manipulative behavior may produce a period of painful estrangement, but hopefully, in the long run, their decision to no longer submit to his bullying would give their in*timid*ated [look at the root of that word!] daughter the strength to do the same."

Samurais Become Their Own Heroes

I'm not the heroic type. I was beaten up by Quakers.
—Woody Allen

You may be thinking, "I hate confrontation. I don't know if I have what it takes to take on a bully." I assure you, you do have what it takes to become a Verbal Samurai—once you decide you will no longer allow anyone to intimidate you and your loved ones. You don't have to be loud or obnoxious, just firm and clear. The following chapters show how to do that so you can fend for yourself and free yourself from people who are trying to beat you up emotionally.

Action Plan and Discussion Questions

Do you have someone in your life who is trying to own you? What are two specific things he or she does to try to lord over you? _____

_____

_____

What do you think of this concept of being a Verbal Samurai? Do you see it as a viable alternative to being a wimp or going on the warpath? Explain. _____

_____

_____

Has a bully forced you into an untenable situation where your only options appear to be lose-lose? Describe that situation. _____

_____

_____

Has he or she in*timid*ated you into being too timid to speak up? How so? _____

_____

_____

Do you understand it's your responsibility to garner the strength to speak up and put an end to the bullying? Are you ready to become your own hero? Explain. _____

_____

_____

Summary

HARMFUL BELIEFS/BEHAVIORS	HELPFUL BELIEFS/BEHAVIORS
This person owns me *"I hate it when my spouse insults me in public, but there's nothing I can do about it."*	I am my own person *"No one has the right to insult me, and I am not going to allow it."*
Belong to a master *"I don't dare say anything. She will get angry if I complain."*	Become a self-master *"I am going to speak up and let her know this is not okay."*
Silently submit to abuse *"I don't want to cause a scene; people might look at us."*	Samurai stops abuse *"I'm going to hold her accountable so she doesn't do this again."*
Lose control and attack back *"I hate it when you do that. Why do you have to be so cruel?"*	Maintain control and stop attack *"Cut it out. Keep those kinds of remarks to yourself."*
Timidly endure mistreatment *"She ruined my whole evening. I'm sorry we even went out."*	Insist on fair treatment *"Speak to me with respect from now on."*

Way 6. Get Out of My Space

I believe each individual is naturally entitled to do as he pleases
with himself and the fruit of his labor, so far as it in no way
interferes with any other man's rights.
—ABRAHAM LINCOLN

BULLIES DO JUST THE OPPOSITE OF WHAT LINCOLN SUGGESTED.
They feel entitled to do exactly as they please even if it interferes with other's rights. In fact, they deliberately invade our
boundaries in an effort to establish dominance. That's why we
need to assert ourselves and back bullies out of our physical and
psychological space. They will continue to push us around if
we don't.

You may be thinking, "Easier said than done. Someone violating my space is such an abstract concept. What space? Is
there a way to make this gray issue more black and white?"
Matter of fact, yes. Read on.

Don't Crowd Me

The tyrant crowds those he can't contol, confuses those he can't
convince, and crushes those he can't corrupt.
—ANONYMOUS

Every animal (including humans) has a safety circle. This is
both a physical and psychological space around us that is ours.
If another animal (including humans) encroaches upon that
imaginary yet real boundary, s/he is too close for comfort.
S/he now poses a threat and we feel at risk.

Wild animals (lions, deer, zebras) and domestic animals (dogs,
cats, horses) have clarity about not letting others violate their
boundaries (as the next story shows). For a variety of reasons,
we human beings frequently allow others to breach our physical and psychological boundaries, and therein lies the problem.

Many times, when someone is behaving in ways that are not
right, fair, or kind, it's because we have not explained or
enforced our boundaries. This chapter explains how to figure
out what and where our boundaries are, and then the rest of the
book explains a variety of ways to protect those boundaries so
we don't get intruded upon.

One of the best examples of boundary enforcement I've ever
witnessed happened one morning while I was walking my Jack
Russell terrier (known for their feistiness) to the beach. JR
spied a cute little furball ahead and dashed up to check her out.
This little doggie dynamo, less than half of JR's size, launched
herself at him and yapped forcefully.

JR jumped back in surprise. The little Pekingese stood there
glowering at him. JR decided to give it another go. He
approached, a little more cautiously this time, to try to sniff
noses (or whatever). She was having none of it. She lunged at
him again with even louder barking. JR got the point and bid
her adieu.

Establish the Pekingese Precedent

> It's not the size of the dog in the fight,
> it's the size of the fight in the dog.
> —DWIGHT D. EISENHOWER

Notice that little Pekingese didn't rationalize JR's behavior with "Well, he probably had a dysfunctional puppyhood and doesn't know any better." She didn't passively submit while reflecting, "Well, he's young and just hasn't learned his doggie manners yet." She didn't pardon his unwelcome approach with "I need to put myself in his tracks and see it from his point of view." She didn't mull over his actions and acquiesce resignedly with "Well, he's probably feeling needy because he's new to the neighborhood and doesn't have any friends."

No, that little furball let JR know in no uncertain terms that his behavior was not welcome. She was quite clear that he had crossed the line, and barking was her way of communicating "Back off!" which JR promptly did.

If only we humans were as clear about barking (I mean marking) our boundaries. Many people in my seminars share tales of woe about bullies who have behaved atrociously. When I ask, "Have you said anything to them about this?" a surprising number admit they haven't.

Unlike the fuzzball, we sometimes rationalize a bully's unwelcome intrusions with "He must have had a frustrating day," "She didn't mean it," or "He's under a lot of pressure." We silently submit to unwanted impositions out of some mixed-up sense of social obligation or fear. We internalize our dismay, thinking, "I can't believe he or she did that!" These are indirect and ineffective paths to protecting our rights. You've heard the phrase "His bark was worse than his bite"? If we bark, we usually won't have to bite because bullies will back off and stop bothering us.

What to Do When Someone Invades Your Safety Circle

> When everyone possesses an individual territory, the
> reasons for one man to dominate another disappear.
> —ROBERT SOMMER IN *PERSONAL SPACE*

Our physical space is an arm's length away, literally. Stretch your arms out in front of you, to the side, and then as far as you can behind you. That's about three feet, and that's your safety circle. People shouldn't come into that "hula hoop" of space unless you invite them in or unless they're someone you trust who has permission to be in close proximity. And yes, the size of personal space varies with different cultures and changes when we're jammed together in a public place. That's why people who are on a packed bus or subway car often avert their eyes. It's a way of honoring others' space and maintaining your own.

From now on, if someone inappropriately crowds you, don't internalize your discomfort, express it with body language or articulate it with words. Raising your eyebrows and looking at the person questioningly is a way of saying, "Yes?" Your body language is sending the unspoken message of "What do you want and what are you doing in my space?" If the person doesn't back away, look rather pointedly at his or her feet and then up, which silently says, "Little close, aren't you?"

If the person still doesn't get the hint, take a step back to reestablish a proper distance. If someone approaches you from behind and looks over your shoulder, turn toward him or her, tilt your head forward while cocking it to one side, engage the person with your eyes, and lift your eyebrows. This is a way of saying, "There must be a reason you're squeezing me. What is it?"

Physical Intimidation Is Not to Be Taken Lightly

Art, like morality, consists of drawing the line somewhere.
—G. K. CHESTERTON

People who violate our boundaries may be doing so innocently. However, if we don't establish from the beginning that *we* control our space, not them, they will conclude they can intrude anytime they want. When we don't determine who can get "near and dear," we abdicate our power. Ethical people won't take advantage of this, but unethical people will. Allowing people to trespass when we don't want them to sends a sign that we can be pushed around and acts as an unfortunate precedent that people can have their way with us.

If someone continues to physically pressure you, use your words in addition to your body language. Hold your hand up toward him or her with your palm out. This is a universal gesture meaning "Stop!" An outstretched hand staves off unwanted advances because it means "Don't come any further." Say out loud, "Hey, give me some room here," or "Whoa, back off a little." This lets people know that you will not passively acquiesce to any attempt to dominate you.

You Conclude Who Can Intrude

My wife and I had words. But I never got to use mine.
—FIBBER McGEE

A woman in a seminar said, "I belong to a professional organization where members go overboard with the hugging. I'm not a prude, but I don't like people I hardly know running up and wrapping their arms around me." Another woman added,

"Yeah. I work with a couple of guys who seem to find any excuse to put their hands on me. They pat me on the shoulder when they compliment me, touch me to say hi as they walk by, and guide me through doors with their hand on my back. It's all supposedly innocent, but I don't like it."

I said to these women, "*You* have the right to decide who touches your body, when, and under what conditions. Social convention is not the priority here. What matters is what you are comfortable with. *You* get to choose who you let into your physical space. It is presumptuous for anyone to assume a physical intimacy that you have not approved. Instead of going along with unrequested physical affection, let people know your preferences. You don't have to be rude, just be clear.

When someone at a meeting starts toward you with that "You're about to get a big bear hug" look, stretch your arm straight out (keep it a little rigid if you have to) to indicate your preference for shaking hands instead. If someone touches you inappropriately, look him or her in the eye and say, "I'd rather you not do that" or "Please keep your hands to yourself." You can say this with a smile if this is a first offense and if you perceive the action to be friendly in nature. Or you can say this with a "Don't do it again" warning voice if he or she has done this before or you perceive the intrusion has unwanted sexual overtones. What's important is that this person now knows you protect your territory and s/he will not be able to trespass at will.

How Can We Tell When Someone
Invades Our Emotional Space?

Being kind doesn't mean one has to be a mat.
—MAYA ANGELOU

It's easy to tell when someone is physically crowding us. It's harder to tell when someone's mentally crowding us. You may be wondering if there's a way to make this "cross the line" concept more concrete.

Yes, there is. From now on, if you sense that someone is trying to overpower you, picture an old-fashioned seesaw like the one you used to play on in the schoolyard. Imagine yourself on one end and the person you're dealing with on the other end. Understand that the success of any relationship (whether it's between you and a friend, you and your spouse, you and your boss, you and whomever) depends on whether this Rights/Needs Seesaw is kept in balance.

Keep a Balance of Power with the Rights/Needs Seesaw

Cooperation means doing what I tell you to do and doing it quick.
—ELBERT HUBBARD, AMERICAN HUMORIST

You've heard the expression that "every relationship has its ups and downs"? That's true, and as long as the ups and downs are *fairly even* (catch the significance of those words), this remains a mutually rewarding relationship. As long as both people are sensitive to each other's wishes, as long as both are willing to make the adjustments that are part of living or working with someone, as long as their compromises are somewhat equitable, and as long as both have equal say about how the ride operates, this will be a healthy partnership.

Rights/Needs Seesaw with an Inbalance of Power

Rights/Needs Seesaw with a Balance of Power

Bullies Don't Want an Equal Ride, They Want to Rule the Ride

I'm really easy to get along with once you learn to see it my way.
—INTERNET JOKE

Bullies don't want a partnership with a balance of power; they want a dictatorship where they have all the power. Their idea of give-and-take is for them to take, take, take while we give, give, give. They drown us in what I call "demands and demeans" so they can be on top of the situation—and us.

Demands are designed to control us. *Demeans* are designed to weaken us. Both are designed to dominate us. Sample demands are demanding your attention while they monopolize every conversation, and demanding your obedience by making decisions for you and giving you hell if you dare disagree. Sample demeans include belittling statements—for example, "No one would ever hire you. You are worthless"—designed to make you doubt yourself. Every aggressive act or manipulative maneuver is designed to diminish your dominion and expand theirs.

Picture your relationship with a domineering individual in your life. Do you have equal say-so about how your ride (relationship) operates, or are you stuck on the bottom all the time? Do you hardly ever get your way and the other person almost always gets his/her way? Do you feel like you're along for the ride, whether you like it or not?

Can you picture how wrong it is for one person in a relationship to always be in the driver's seat? Can you see that it's appropriate for you to get your fair share of needs/rights met? Do you understand that bullies will do everything in their power to put you down and keep you down? From now on, when a tyrant tries to dictate circumstances, vow to stand up for what's fair despite his/her efforts to topple you.

Don't Forgive Bullies Their Trespasses

In life, as in a football game, the principle to follow is: hit the line hard; don't foul and don't shirk, but hit the line hard!
—THEODORE ROOSEVELT

If someone is invading your space, don't shirk responsibility; take responsibility and hit the line hard enough to convince this trespasser to back off.

A manager named Norm said, "I have an employee who drives me nuts. Tracy is always complaining about something. She comes in late, leaves early, and is always asking for time off to run errands she insists can't wait until after work. In the beginning, I agreed to her requests, but after a while it got to be too much and the other employees resented that she was getting special treatment.

"Tracy walked into my office last week and told me she was planning to attend a networking luncheon on Friday. Normally, I support employees who want to participate in industry programs. However, I thought this was just another one of her ploys to get out of the office.

"I mentally pictured the history of her demands over the last few months. It was obvious that she had taken more than her fair share of favors. I told her she couldn't go, that she was behind on her projects and needed to get caught up. She tried to get me to change my mind by saying it was too late to cancel because she had already paid. I told her she could give the ticket to someone else or get a credit for a future event, but that she was needed in the office all day Friday.

"She was not used to not getting her way. She accused me of not supporting her professional development. Instead of responding to that ludicrous claim, I stayed on track and said, 'Tracy, *you* are the one who has repeatedly taken time off and not made up for it. It's time you fulfill your work obligations.' She stormed out of my office, but I didn't budge and didn't apologize because I was clear that she was the one out of line, not me."

Samurais Live in a State of Resolve, Not a State of Resignation

Until I knew I could ask for what I wanted, I had lived my life
in an unacknowledged state of resignation. I had silently
agreed not to be a nuisance, to never intrude on or take
up anyone's time, and certainly not to be a pest.
—JACK CANFIELD

From now on, resolve not to let other people be a nuisance. Picture your safety circle and the Rights/Needs Seesaw and vow not to let bullies intrude on your space or pester you with over-the-top demands and demeans. You may be thinking, "I agree with this in theory; how do I do this in practice?" That's next.

Action Plan and Discussion Questions

Has someone in your life been intruding on your physical space? How so? _____

_____

_____

_____

What's a good example of boundary enforcement that you've witnessed? Describe what happened when this person or animal established the Pekingese Precedent. _____

_____

_____

_____

What are *you* going to do the next time a trespasser gets too close for comfort? _____

_____

_____

Who is someone in your life who tries to dominate you with demands and demeans? What has she or he been doing or saying? _____

_____

_____

Picture the Rights/Needs Seesaw with two significant others in your life. Are the ups and downs fairly equal? Is one of you on top and one on bottom most of the time? Explain.

_____

_____

_____

Do you agree that it is your right to conclude who intrudes? What is one specific thing you are going to do to keep bullies from abusing your psychological boundaries? _____

_____

_____

Summary

HARMFUL BELIEFS/BEHAVIORS	HELPFUL BELIEFS/BEHAVIORS
Bullies physically crowd us *"I don't like it when Jill gets right in my face like this."*	We protect our safety circle *"Jill, back up and give me some room here."*
Bullies put us down *"I can't believe she's asking to borrow more money."*	We stand up for ourselves *"No, Jill, you'll have to get that loan from someone else."*
Bullies demand to control us *"I still haven't been paid the money I lent you before."*	We aren't sidetracked by demands *"Before you ask for more cash, let's talk about the thousand bucks I'm owed."*
Bullies demean to weaken us *"I am not stingy! Here, take the cash."*	We don't give in to manipulation *"Jill, you're not getting any money."*
Bullies pressure us until we're resigned to our fate *"What do you mean, you want to borrow my car, too?"*	We are resolved to protect our time, space, and fate *"When you've repaid the loan, we can talk about you using my car."*

Way 7. Be Positively Intolerant

I hate people who are intolerant.
—LAURENCE J. PETER, CANADIAN AUTHOR

DID YOU GROW UP IN THE SIXTIES OR SEVENTIES? WAS YOUR motto "Let It Be" or "Live and Let Live"? Did you listen to songs that suggested you "Love the One You're With"? Tolerance is indeed an admirable trait. Intolerance can also be an admirable trait.

What? This was demonstrated to me while I was attending a convention presenters' dinner. On my right was a screenwriter-agent from Los Angeles, and on my left was a self-described Southern belle who had helped organize the conference. We were discussing the not-too-impressive lot of movies that had been released over the last few months. The woman on my left decried the decline of values and then added, almost as an afterthought, "A lot of this is the fault of all those homosexuals in Hollywood."

The screenwriter and I both blinked, not sure we had heard what we had just heard. I was offended by her remark, but was prepared to overlook her offensive remark. The agent wasn't going to let her off so easy. He looked at her in amazement and asked, "What did you say?" She realized she had overstepped her boundaries and quickly backpedaled. He made one more comment about how inappropriate her observation had been and then moved the topic on to something else.

I remember thinking, "Good for him." He was absolutely right *not* to let it be. Hopefully, expressing his intolerance of her sweeping generalization will make her think twice about her homophobic remark. She may even decide that not only will she not say anything like this anymore, she won't think it anymore either.

Don't Go Along for the Deride

Arguing with my wife is like this: "I came, I saw, I concurred."
—COFFEE MUG SLOGAN

That's the power of positive intolerance. We don't want to concur when people abuse our emotional space with inappropriate remarks. My son Andrew and I were doing the weekly laundry and we were tossing clothes into the washing machine. Andrew came in with an armload of basketball T-shirts and casually remarked, "Oh, yeah, Mom, I need some more 'wifebeaters.'" I looked at him, stunned, and asked disbelievingly, "What?"

He explained, "Wife-beaters. You know, the shirts with the cut-off sleeves you wear under your basketball jersey." I told him, "Andrew, that term is offensive to me."

He answered, "But, Mom, that's what everyone calls them." I responded, "Andrew, other people may call them that. The question is, are you proud of calling them that? Is that the kind of term you feel good using? Please think of some other name for them." He nodded and easily agreed, "Okay, Mom."

If I had said nothing, Andrew would have thought nothing

of continuing to use that offensive phrase. Please commit this to memory: *When people say or do something that offends you, if you don't let them know it, they will continue saying and doing things that offend you.* After all, you didn't protest, so it must be all right, right?

Offensive Behavior That Goes Unchallenged Gets Repeated

If we don't stand for something, we'll fall for anything.
—ANN LANDERS

From now on, resolve to keep these "positively intolerant" responses at the ready so you can stop people in their verbal tracks if they say something loathsome:

- "Keep those kinds of thoughts to yourself."
- "You might want to reconsider that. It doesn't reflect well on you."
- "You can't mean that."
- "Do you want to repeat that?" (said incredulously with raised eyebrows)
- "I'm sure I didn't hear that right. Do you want to rephrase that?"
- "Don't say stuff like that when you're with me."
- "Use different language. That is unacceptable."
- "What makes you think I want to listen to that?"

Take Note

A memorandum is written not to inform the reader
but to protect the writer.
—DEAN ACHESON

The above phrases can convince garbage mouths (as my mom used to call them) to change their tasteless tune. There is another, even more tangible way to persuade people to clean up their off-color act. I used this technique at an airport and can vouch for its effectiveness.

My delayed flight landed after midnight. The complimentary hotel shuttle bus had stopped running, so I needed to catch a cab, even though my hotel was only five minutes away. I got in the backseat and gave the driver my destination. As soon as he heard the name of the hotel, he went ballistic and started swearing a blue streak.

I knew why he was upset. He had probably waited in line for an hour and was hoping to get a fifty-dollar fare, not a five-dollar fare. I understood his frustration, but screaming obscenities was not an option. Someone spewing profanity at you is a clear case of verbal abuse. Instead of yelling back at him, I simply pulled paper and pen from my purse, leaned over the front seat to look at his driver's license, and asked pointedly, "How do you spell your name?"

He stopped, mid (invective-filled) sentence, and drove the rest of the way in silence. As soon as we arrived at my hotel, he jumped out and came over to open my door. He took my hand in his and pleaded, "Please don't report me. I can't afford to lose my license." He was as contrite as could be, and I marveled at the simple effectiveness of asking someone how to spell their name.

From now on, if people vent their vitriol at you, don't verbally lie down and take it. If you suspect this is a rare overreaction, you may choose to first use a sympathetic "Has it been

one of those days?" Your caring question may be just the thing
to let them know you're on their side and they'll stop directing
their rage at you. If they don't respond to your attempts to
work things out, you might want to make a last-ditch win-win
effort with, "This has been upsetting for both of us, and I'm
sure we can resolve it if we focus on solutions, not fault."

If they continue to rant or if you are simply not willing to tolerate their outburst, take out paper and pen and ask pointedly,
"How do you spell your name?" or "What was that you said?"
Rather than becoming belligerent yourself, these simple questions let them know their verbal abuse is not going to be
allowed. Making a memo is a way to inform insolent individuals
you are making a written record of their inappropriate remarks,
which is often sufficient incentive for them to zip their lip.

Are You Up to the Test?

> Where laws end, tyranny begins.
> —WILLIAM PITT

Understand that people who act objectionably are in a way
testing you to see what they can get away with. That's why it's
so important to establish and enforce boundaries in the beginning of any relationship. Teachers know the importance of
starting the school year tough. As my aunt Carol, who was a
kindergarten teacher in California for more than twenty years,
said, "You can always loosen up as time goes by. But if you
don't let 'em know who's boss that first day, you'll be playing
catch-up the rest of the semester."

Consider what Aunt Carol said: "We've got to let them know
who's boss." *Boss* is defined as "one who exercises authority or
control." That is why bullies come on so strong. They're trying
to establish themselves as top dog. If we allow would-be bullies
to boss us around, we'll end up as the underdog.

Who's the Boss?

I have my standards. They may be low, but I have them.
—BETTE MIDLER

The first day of class, Aunt Carol always laid down the laws. One of the most important rules was that when she clapped her hands three times, everyone was to get silent immediately. She would practice with the class until everyone, and I mean everyone, got it right. "Right" meant no talking: not one giggle, whisper, or tailing-off conversation. Those five-year-olds respected Aunt Carol because they knew they were loved and would be held accountable for courteous behavior. Aunt Carol didn't believe in wishy-washy rules that were enforced one day and not the next, applied to one child and not the other. Her standards (boundaries for behavior) were clearly stated and consistently enforced. As a result, there was order in the classroom and those kindergartners behaved like angels (well, most of the time).

Do you have standards of behavior for the people in your life? Are they too low or inconsistently enforced? If so, it's not too late to declare a do-over. Remember do-overs from when you were growing up? Do-overs are the child's equivalent of a golfer's mulligan. Perhaps you were playing jump rope, and three jumps in, you slipped and stepped on the rope. "Do over?" you asked hopefully.

Declare a Do-Over

He turned his life around. He used to be depressed and miserable.
Now he's miserable and depressed.
—ROBERT FROST

A woman named Carla said her husband had gotten into the habit of coming home in a black mood. He'd slam the door on the way in, throw his briefcase on the table, and stomp around the house until his funk wore off. Anyone unlucky enough to get in his way got an earful.

"I put up with it for a long time because he worked in a golden-handcuff job that he hated but couldn't afford to leave because it paid so well. On top of that, he spent at least an hour commuting each way, so I thought he deserved some slack.

"After years of this, it occurred to me that *I* had bad days at work, too, and I didn't take it out on everyone else. Sometimes the kids were upset about something that happened at school and they didn't think it gave them the right to make everyone else miserable. I decided we'd had enough. That evening George made his normal grumpy entrance. I picked up his briefcase, took him by the arm, and marched him back outside. I closed the screen door in his face and announced, 'We're tired of you being such a grouch. We have bad days, too, and we don't take it out on you. From now on, when you walk into our home, treat us with the courtesy we deserve and leave your rotten moods outside.'" She said with a smile, "He got the point."

What Do We Do with Customers Who Are Out of Line?

Tolerance is only another name for indifference.
—W. SOMERSET MAUGHAM

A public seminar audience got into a heated debate about what we should do if we're dealing with a customer who won't respond to reason. A financial consultant contributed her opinion: "At my first job, the rule was 'The customer is always right.' That may work in theory. However, it doesn't always work in practice. We deal with some very demanding clients who seem to think they can treat us any way they want. My mother and father taught me I have the right to be treated with respect, and that doesn't include having someone order me around like a servant.

"One of our VIP clients launched into a tirade over the phone one day because she wasn't happy with how her investments were performing. I listened patiently for a while, sympathized about the market downturn, and then tried to focus on what action we could take. She continued using me as her personal wailing wall. I finally interrupted and said, 'Mrs.____ (who shall remain nameless), I want to help you, and please speak to me with respect.' She continued calling me every name in the book. I said it one more time. She kept venting, so I ended the conversation with 'Mrs.____, I want this conversation to be productive, and it's not. I am going to hang up, and you are welcome to call back when you are ready to speak to us with respect.'

"I knew there was a chance she would call our branch manager to complain about my impertinence, so I quickly documented the call so my supervisor would know what she had said and why I responded the way I did. She did call to complain, and thankfully our manager backed me up."

Open Your Mind to Intolerance

An open mind is all very well in its way, but it ought not to be so open that there is no keeping anything in or out of it. It should be capable of shutting its doors, sometimes.
—SAMUEL BUTLER

A savings and loan officer said, "I agree with this. Our policy is that the customer is right most of the time, but not always. We give our employees the right to make judgment calls about over-the-line behavior. We have an unwritten policy that our workers do not have to tolerate extreme behavior. We're even willing to lose a client if they insist on abusing a staff member. I got a call from one of our tellers who was being browbeaten by a customer. This teller, Lynne, has worked for us for years and is unfailingly polite. I knew the client must have really been a tough customer if Lynne hadn't been able to win him over. I asked that the man be put on the phone and started with my usual 'How can I help you?' combined with 'I'm sure we can work this out.'

"Most people calm down with that line because they feel they're talking to a senior employee who has the power to resolve their situation. It also helps that I assert the belief that we'll be able to come to a satisfactory conclusion.

"It didn't work with this customer. He continued ranting and raving. I kept trying to steer the conversation to a solution, but he was having none of it. After ten minutes of futility, I interrupted and said, 'Sir, it seems like we're not going to be able to satisfy you today. If you'd like to give the phone back to the teller, I will ask her to draw up a cashier's check for the amount in your account, and you are welcome to find a financial institution that fits your needs.'

"He sputtered a few times and then admitted, 'I don't want to close my account.' 'Fine, then,' I told him. 'Let's focus on how we can settle this issue and move forward.' That worked with him, but there are some people who refuse to respond to reason. I tell employees it's okay to 'fire' a client who repeatedly refuses to cooperate. I trust their judgment. I would rather they spent their time servicing our thousands of satisfied customers than spent all day trying to turn around a permanently disgruntled 'I'm going to be difficult until the day I die' individual."

Intolerance Can Be Risky Business

Toleration is a good thing in its place; but you cannot tolerate what will not tolerate you, and is trying to cut your throat.
—JAMES FROUD

Are you dealing with an "I'm going to be difficult until the day I die" individual? Freya Stark said, "Tolerance cannot afford to have anything to do with the fallacy that evil may convert itself to good." Understand that intolerance can be a good thing if it is used so that evildoers cannot use you for target practice.

Be sure to consider the consequences *before* you shoot from the lip and confront a volatile person. Intolerance can carry risks. I don't want to give the impression that every encounter with a bully winds up with a happy ending. Way 14, "Know When to Hold 'Em, When to Fold 'Em" features a checklist that can help us decide when to persist to resist—and when it's in our best interests to cease and desist.

Have you noticed a trend in these positively intolerant responses? They use the word *you* instead of the word *I*. This contradicts everything you've learned about assertiveness, doesn't it? The next chapter explains why "owning" your reaction creates a verbal backlash with bullies.

Action Plan and Discussion Questions

Do you know someone who has a history of spewing preju- diced, bigoted, or sexist remarks? What have you done about it in the past? _____

_____

_____

How are you going to practice "positive intolerance" from now on? What are you going to say the next time someone makes an intolerable remark? _____

_____

_____

Can you think of a time when you documented someone's inappropriate behavior? Did it convince them to cease and desist? Explain. _____

_____

_____

Were you taught that the customer is always right? Do you agree with that? What are some exceptions? _____

_____

_____

Do you have a client or customer who is behaving intolera- bly? Are you prepared to hold them accountable even if that means "firing" them? Explain. _____

_____

_____

Summary

HARMFUL BELIEFS/BEHAVIORS	HELPFUL BELIEFS/BEHAVIORS
Love the one you're with, and live and let live *"It makes me uncomfortable when Dad makes those Archie Bunker types of remarks. Oh, well."*	Love the one you're with and live and let live if they deserve it *"I love you, Dad, and please keep those kind's of remarks to yourself when we're around."*
Let it be *"It's Christmas. I don't want to spoil our annual get-together."*	Don't let bigotry be *"This happens every year. If I don't talk to him about it, it's going to keep happening."*
Say nothing, so they think nothing of continuing *"Hey, Dad, what'd you think of the football game?"*	Protest so they know it's not okay to continue *"Dad, can I talk with you for a minute on the back porch?"*
Take offense when someone swears a blue streak *"I don't deserve to be talked to that way."*	Take notes when someone swears a blue streak *"Excuse me, how do you spell your name?"*

Way 8. Respond to the Strategy, Not the Substance

There is no defense against reproach but obscurity.
—JOSEPH ADDISON

ACTUALLY, THE BEST DEFENSE AGAINST REPROACH IS TO RESPOND with "you" rather than "I." This is one of the most important insights to keep in mind when dealing with someone who uses criticism to control. Bullies float trial-balloon taunts to get a reaction. Often they don't believe what they're saying; they're just saying it to get a rise out of you. They like to stir things up and watch you stew because it's a power trip for them.

From now on, ignore intentionally inflammatory attacks and address the tactic behind them. Denying an outrageous accusation with "I never said that!" or "That's not true!" rewards bullies, because we are now debating their dubious point. Responding to a reproach with an "I reply," even if we deny what they've said, means that they've successfully engaged us in an argument.

Address the *Intent*, Not the *Content* of
Taunts and Tirades

I'd like to say I'm glad you're here. I'd like to say it.
—HENNY YOUNGMAN

If you're dealing with someone who likes to throw out disparaging remarks, lob the verbal hot potato right back in his/her lap. If someone says huffily, "Well, this is a technical issue and I'm not going to waste my time explaining it to you because you're not smart enough to understand it," interrupt and say, "What did you just say to me?" and then stop talking.

Making people repeat their snotty remark lets them know they're not going to get away with their insult. This simple question puts *them* on the spot instead of you. The query "What did you just say to me?" forces verbal hit–and–run artists to explain themselves and lets them know you're not going along for their deride.

Cut 'Em Off at the Pass . . . ive Aggressive Remark

I don't want to be patronizing—that means talking down.
—WENDY MORGAN

While I was out shopping for groceries, a man named Rob who had attended a Tongue Fu! workshop walked up, beaming, and reported a success story. He explained, "I work with a guy who seems to go out of his way to be condescending. I've been on the job longer, but he's got the higher degree and rubs his academic credentials in my face at every opportunity. The Monday after your workshop, Jack walked up to my desk, looked over my shoulder at a project I was working on, and said loud enough so everyone in our office could hear, 'Having trouble with that spreadsheet? You really should try college. They teach that in your freshman year.'

"That did it," Rob said. "He had humiliated me in public for the last time. I stood up and got right in his face and said, 'What did you just say to me?' You should have seen him. His mouth dropped open and he just stared at me in shock. I don't think anyone had ever challenged him before. I didn't say anything else; I didn't have to. I just kept looking at him, waiting for an answer. He finally mumbled something under his breath and beat a hasty retreat."

Bravo. Another reason the phrase "What did you just say to me?" works so well is because it uses the word *you* instead of the word *I*. "Doing the You," as in "Looks like *you're* up to your old tricks" or "*You're* not trying to pull that again, are you?" puts the responsibility ball back in the bully's court where it belongs. By responding to the *intent* of the remark rather than its *essence*, you expose the bully's little game.

Do the You

> You go Uruguay and I'll go mine.
> —GROUCHO MARX

By all means, continue to use "I replies" when dealing with individuals who have a conscience. If we use "I replies" with people who *don't* have a conscience, though, they'll laugh in our face. Telling bullies "*I* don't like how you're behaving" doesn't motivate them to quit, it motivates them to continue. They want us to dislike what they're doing.

Furthermore, bullies already try to make us own their misdeeds. Using an "I reply" boomerangs back on us because it plays right into their strategy to keep us on the defensive and them on the offensive. "Doing the You" keeps the attention where it belongs—on the bully's inappropriate conduct. Imagine someone is calling you names. Saying, "*I* don't like it when you do that" makes *your* reaction the problem. "Doing the You," saying "Keep those kind of comments to yourself," deflects verbal arrows and keeps them from penetrating your boundary.

Get You'sed to Using You

> I only open my mouth to change feet.
> —EMILY PAINE

Using "you" instead of "I" may feel awkward and may even sound wrong initially because it's different. That's why I've provided a variety of "I Replies" and "Do the You" responses so you can practice making the switch. You may even want to say these phrases out loud so you get comfortable with this new communication technique. Rehearsing these responses can help them roll off your tongue so you don't put your foot in your mouth when it's time to use them in real life. As you say them out loud, listen to yourself and hear how the "I Replies" would come across as whiny to an aggressor checking you out for weakness. The "Do the You" responses work because they rebuff his/her attempts to intimidate you.

"I REPLIES"	"DO THE YOU" RESPONSES
"I want you to stop bothering me."	"You need to back off."
"I've had enough."	"You have gone too far."
"I don't appreciate having to wait."	"You need to apologize for being late."

"I don't think that's very nice."	"Clean up your act."
"I don't like to be called names."	"Your calling me names isn't going to change my mind."
"I'm uncomfortable with being rushed."	"You'll get my answer in the morning."

Don't Settle for Less

The minute you settle for less than you deserve,
you get even less than you settled for.
—MAUREEN DOWD

The minute we settle for unacceptable behavior, we get even more than we bargained for. As my friend says, "Give 'em an inch, and they'll think they're a ruler."

A disc jockey at an Arizona radio station shared a "Do the You" success story. Following our in-studio interview, this deejay, who had been in a wheelchair for most of his adult life, told me about the rather frightening time he had had when firing an employee. "This guy was really upset. He stormed into my office and lit into me. He was leaning over, shaking his fist in my face. Instead of backing down in the face of his threats, I looked him in the eye and said, 'We'll have this conversation as soon as you sit down in that chair.'

"I was kind of surprised, but he sat down. If I had said something like 'I don't like being yelled at,' he would have probably shouted back, 'Tough! I don't like being fired' and kept letting me have it."

This deejay was right. An "I Reply" would have made him come across as a wimp. "Doing the You"—that is to say, "You need to speak to me with respect"—commanded the employee's compliance because it was a command instead of a cowardly plea. The deejay's strong rather than sympathetic response was exactly what the situation called for.

Don't Be a Doormat When Being Dominated

> You gotta take the sour with the bitter.
> —MAL HANCOCK

One woman had a problem with this idea. She said, "Isn't this just attacking back? They always say that violence leads to more violence. Won't an aggressive response lead to more aggression?"

Good question. Surprisingly, some people won't be sour, bitter, or angry when you hold them accountable for their over-the-line behavior, they'll be grateful. Some individuals who are stepping on your emotional toes are actually unaware of their offensive behavior. It's like the T shirt I saw on a teenager that read: "Help, I'm talking and I can't stop." Some people don't have the discipline to monitor their own behavior, they expect you to monitor it for them. They figure if you don't like how they're acting, it's up to you to do something about it.

This was the situation with Nina, who told me, "My cousin was downsized when her corporation was acquired in a merger. In the course of one week, the company line changed from 'Don't worry, your job is secure' to 'We're going to have to reduce the workforce by half' to 'Sorry, but your department has been abolished.'"

Nina continued. "My cousin called almost every night to report her latest job-search nightmare. At first my heart went out to her because I imagined how awful it must have been to go from employed to unemployed through no fault of your own. As the weeks went by, though, I got a little fed up with her nightly calls. She seemed to feel I didn't have anything better to do than to listen to her gripe. I finally left my answering machine on and didn't take her calls. I know that wasn't very nice, but I was tired of listening to her. How should I have handled it?"

I suggested she could have pictured the Rights/Needs Seesaw to see that it wasn't rude to let her cousin know her nightly calls were over the top, it was the correct thing to do. Instead of avoiding the issue—which rarely solves the problem and often aggravates it—she could have put a stop to the free therapy by saying, "I'm really sorry about what happened, and I'll be glad to help you brainstorm how to find a new job. I'm not willing to listen to you rehash how unfair this all is. That's not helping either of us."

Don't Agonize; Articulate

> To jaw-jaw is always better than to war-war.
> —SIR WINSTON CHURCHILL

To jaw-jaw is better than to ignore-ignore. Nina got back in touch with me to report that she did contact her cousin, who much to Nina's surprise admitted that it hadn't been fair to hog Nina's evenings and apologized. Nina said, "What an eye-opener. It was so much simpler to just tell her how I felt instead of agonizing over the issue."

Remember Nina's lesson. Many people are glad when we clarify our boundaries because it means they don't have to second-guess how we feel. Honest communication is such a relief because we don't have to wonder if the other person is telling the truth or saying something "just to be nice." Instead of having to read between the lines and worry about hidden agendas, we can take each other at our word. It's a marvelous thing in a relationship to trust that other people will let us know if we're doing something that's bothering them.

People Can't Read Our Minds

Any connection between your reality and mind
is purely coincidental.
—INTERNET JOKE

Remember, we can't expect people to intuit how we feel. Communication can't be left to chance or coincidence. "Doing the You" is a clear way to let others know we consider their behavior objectionable. If they're ethical, they'll appreciate the heads-up. If they're unethical, they'll understand that we won't buy into their taunts, tirades, and power plays.

Ready to lighten up? Our next chapter shares some Quip Pro Quos that we can use if someone is trying to get on our last nerve.

Action Plan and Discussion Questions

Have you been taught to use "I replies" when communicating with others? Do you see how they backfire with people who are already trying to hold you responsible for their behavior? Explain. _____

_____

_____

Who is someone who frequently tries to blame you for what's wrong? How are you going to put the responsibility ball back in his or her court? _____

_____

_____

How are you going to remind yourself to respond to the strategy of demeaning remarks instead of reacting to their substance? _____

_____

_____

Can you think of a verbal hit-and-run artist who floats trial-balloon taunts? What kinds of things does s/he say?_____

_____

_____

Summary

HARMFUL BELIEFS/BEHAVIORS	HELPFUL BELIEFS/BEHAVIORS
Use the word *I* to tell bullies we don't like what they're doing *"I don't think it's very nice of you to say I'm a terrible cook."*	Use the word *you* to tell bullies their behavior is out of line *"If you don't like my cooking, you're welcome to fix your own dinner."*
Focus on our reaction to the bully's behavior *"I spent all afternoon in the kitchen preparing that meal."*	Keep the focus on the bully's behavior *"Next time you want to criticize dinner, you can help make it."*

Wait for bullies to self-examine or self-correct *"Why doesn't he appreciate that I worked all day and compliment me instead of criticize me?"*	Take responsibility for correcting bully behavior *"We could probably have better dinners if you pitched in when you got home."*
Address the essence of accusations *"What do you mean, the meat was overcooked?"*	Address the intent of accusations *"Did you have a terrible day and you're taking it out on me?"*
Respond to the substance of a reproach *"I may not be a gourmet cook, but I did the best I could."*	Respond to the strategy of a reproach *"If you're trying to make me feel bad, it's not going to work."*

Way 9. Beat 'Em to the Punch . . . Line

Perhaps one has to become very old before one learns how
to be amused rather than offended.
—PEARL S. BUCK

WHY WAIT UNTIL WE'RE OLD TO LEARN HOW TO BE AMUSED
rather than offended? Why not learn now? Humor is a time-
tested way to playfully block a bully from having his or her way
with us. Bullies push, push, push to see what we're made of. If
we're able to successfully parry their verbal jabs, they'll usually
leave us alone because they know we're up to the test.

An attorney friend is a perfect practitioner of this concept.
Pam said, "I got sick and tired of hearing all the lawyer jokes. I
know some people have had unsatisfying experiences at the
hands of the legal system. However, it gets old hearing for the
umpteenth time, 'How do you know when a lawyer is lying?
When her lips are moving' and 'What do you call a hundred
lawyers at the bottom of the sea? A good start.' An associate
finally told me that being made fun of comes with the attorney
territory, and I better develop a thick skin or my sensitivity
about this was going to drive me nuts.

"She was right. Now I collect lawyer jokes and post the best ones on a bulletin board in my office. If I'm at a cocktail party and someone starts in with 'Hey, have you heard the one about . . .' instead of inwardly groaning, I add my two cents (two hundred dollars?) worth. One of my favorites is 'Why don't sharks attack lawyers? Professional courtesy.'"

Lighten Up Instead of Tighten Up

> No one becomes a laughingstock who laughs at himself.
> —SENECA

Another example of someone who wisely decided to lighten up instead of tighten up is Joseph Heller. He said, "When I read something saying I've not written anything as good as *Catch-22*, I'm tempted to reply, 'Who has?'" Good for Heller. Heller's *Catch-22* was a masterpiece that included a phrase that has become a watchword of our time. Only a handful of authors have achieved that type of enduring impact on popular culture. Whether he liked it or not, his follow-up books would all be compared (probably unfavorably) to this once-in-a-lifetime novel. It was smart of him to anticipate this public reaction and handle it with aplomb rather than affront.

If You Can't Beat 'Em, Join In

> Blessed are they who can laugh at themselves, for they
> shall never cease to be amused.
> —ANONYMOUS

A man named Art who was "follicly challenged" said he agreed with my friend's decision to not take herself so seriously. He explained, "I started losing my hair when I was only thirty-five years old. I went the rug route and should have taken out stock in Rogaine. After about five years of sinking thousands of dollars into hair plugs and everything else on the market, I realized I was fighting a losing battle (so to speak) and decided I might as well learn to live with and laugh at my baldness. If someone tries to make a joke at my expense, I come right back at 'em with a joke of my own, like 'I'm not losing my hair, I'm gaining face.' Sometimes I say, 'I'm not bald, I'm a man of scalp' or 'I'm not bald, I'm a hair donor.' Once people realize I'm not self-conscious about it, it takes the fun out of it for them and they usually drop it."

Art had a good point. When bullies discover their goads don't get our goat, they go elsewhere. Their goal is to make you feel embarrassed. If you're not bothered by their verbal darts, they'll stop slinging them because they're pointless.

Quip Pro Quo

Humor is just another defense against the universe.
—MEL BROOKS

A lot of articles and books tell you to use humor to defuse a bully's verbal grenade; they just don't tell you how. What exactly are we supposed to say when bullies zero in on our emotional sore spots? How can we keep the cat from getting our tongue? I wanted to put my "funny" where my mouth is, so I've provided a variety of Quip Pro Quos (wisecracks) you can use to defend yourself the next time someone tries to step on your mental toes.

DIVORCE:
"Why did you get a divorce?"
"Let's just put it this way. We had five years of happy marriage, but we were married for fifteen."—Bob Thomas

SINGLE:
"Why isn't a cute young thing like you married?"
"I think, therefore I'm single."—Liz Winstead

AGE:
"How old are you anyway?"
"Let's just say my back goes out more than I do."
—Phyllis Diller

FITNESS:
"Why don't you work out?"
"I'm pushing sixty; that's enough exercise for me."
—Mark Twain

EDUCATION:
"What's your degree in?"
"I have an ND—No Degree!"
"Well, I pursued my degree at Berkeley, but I never caught it."

WEIGHT:
"Wow, you've really packed on the pounds."
"I resemble that remark."—Groucho Marx

UNSOLICITED ADVICE:
"You know what you should have done?"
"When I want your opinion, I'll give it to you."—Madonna

PREGNANT:
"Are you having a baby?" (and you're not pregnant)
"Yeah, I'm having twins. I'm naming them Ben and Jerry."
—Rosie O'Donnell

BAD MEMORY:
"Are you getting senile or something?"
"No, I'm suffering from déjà vu amnesia. I think I've forgotten
this before."—Roseanne Barr

Put Your Funny Where Your Mouth Is

I don't think being funny is anyone's first choice.
—WOODY ALLEN

Being funny with someone who's crossed the courtesy line may not be our first choice, but it's worth a try if everything else we've tried has failed. "The sound of laughter has always seemed to me," observed Peter Ustinov, "the most civilized music in the universe." Sometimes humor is a civilized yet effective way to get through to someone who's not listening.

This was demonstrated by a veterinarian's assistant who told me about her boss's clever handling of a client who wouldn't take no for an answer. This client was a well-known cheapskate who was always questioning her bill. She had called the vet's office because her dog Fifi had hurt her paw and the owner was trying to figure out whether it was serious enough to bring her in. Actually, she was trying to get free advice so she could treat the injury herself instead of having to pay a visit to the clinic.

After ten frustrating minutes of back-and-forth, the vet finally said, "Mabel, put down the phone, go get Fifi, and bring her to the phone." "What?" squawked Mabel. "Just do it," the doctor ordered. So Mabel put down the phone, found Fifi, and brought her back to the phone.

The vet said, "Now hold Fifi up so I can look at her paw and see how bad it is." Mabel protested, "You can't see Fifi's paw over the phone!" The doctor pounced. "That's right, I can't see Fifi's paw over the phone. Now bring her in so I can make a proper diagnosis and we can get this treated." Bravo!

Pun Fu!

> It was so quiet you could hear a pun drop.
> —Anonymous

A friend from Maui shared another marvelous example of someone who had perfected what I call Pun Fu! (a Tongue Fu! technique of handling hassles with humor instead of harsh words). This woman said, "I was on a packed flight from Hawaii to Los Angeles. Every single seat was full, so we were all crammed together elbow to elbow. There was a little boy, probably about five years old, wearing a cowboy hat and cowboy boots running up and down the aisles pretending to shoot passengers with his straw. We all kept looking at the mother, waiting for her to do something about her son. The mother had a baby on her lap and was so busy taking care of her infant, she had obviously given up on the cowboy.

"Finally the senior flight attendant walked over, hunkered down to the little sharpshooter's level, put her hands on his shoulders, looked him in the eye, and said, 'Would you like to play outside?'

"Deer in headlights. The little boy's eyes got this big. He scurried back to his seat, and there he sat for the rest of the flight."

Have You Got Jest Lag?

> Your humor never fails to abuse me.
> —The Lion King

Are you thinking, "But I'm not funny" or "My sense of humor never shows up until it's too late"? Understand the key to thinking on your feet is to brainstorm sensitive scenarios beforehand so you don't go brain-dead when they happen. What are you touchy about? Is there a particular question or comment you dread?

If someone is going for the jugular vein instead of the jocular vein, check out the www.humorproject.com Web site run by Dr. Joel Goodman and Margie Ingram, directors of the Humor Project in Saratoga Springs, New York. This couple believes humor is supposed to be amusing instead of abusing, and they have conferences, seminars, and a warehouse of newsletters, books, and videos that all prove Robin Williams's philosophy that humor is "acting out optimism." Their annual International Conference on Humor and Creativity brings people from all over the world to learn how to laugh *with* each other instead of *at* each other.

Live Happily Ever Laughter

> He laughs best whose laugh lasts.
> —LAURENCE J. PETER

Understand you don't have to reinvent the laughter wheel all by yourself. Ask people in similar situations what they say when their sore subject is brought up. Check out the humor books at your local library, bookstore, or comedy Web site. By researching and acquiring (be sure to attribute and give credit where credit is due) a repertoire of wisecracks in advance, you never again need worry about being tongue-tied when someone's trying to have fun at your expense.

Action Plan and Discussion Questions

What is something you're sensitive about? _____
_____
_____

What do you say if someone brings this up? Are you tongue-tied or do you let loose the retort on the tip of your tongue?
_____
_____

Can you think of any funny Quip Pro Quos you've heard? Do you know people who have developed clever wisecracks for often-asked questions? Who are they, and what do they say? _____
_____
_____

What punch lines are you going to develop so you can handle zaps with poise instead of panic?
_____
_____

Have you witnessed a situation where someone used humor instead of harsh words (Pun Fu!)? What happened? _____
_____
_____

Summary

HARMFUL BELIEFS/BEHAVIORS	HELPFUL BELIEFS/BEHAVIORS
Sensitive about sore spots *"I'm embarrassed that my memory isn't what it used to be."*	Sense of humor about sore spots *"Okay, I can be frustrated by it or I can have fun with it."*
Tighten up *"Oh, I forgot her name again. This is humiliating."*	Lighten up *"I must be suffering from mental-pause. What is your name?"*
Bullies use us as their verbal punching bag *"You must be getting senile or something."*	We beat bullies to the punch . . . line with Quip Pro Quos *"Yeah, I forget three things. Names, birthdays, and I can't remember the third."* —*Henny Youngman*
Suffer from "I should have said" syndrome *"I don't know how I can face her again."*	Brainstorm sensitive situations and prepare Fun Fu! responses *"I have a photographic memory. I just haven't developed it yet."* —Jonathan Winters

Way 10. Look Out for the Telltale Traits of a Tyrant

Actions lie louder than words.
—CAROL WELLS, COMEDIENNE

"IF ONLY I HAD LISTENED TO MY INSTINCTS." KATHY SIGHED. "I HAD never been pursued so ardently. I met Ron at a church retreat. He asked me out the next night, the next night, and the next. By our sixth date, he had asked me to marry him. I hadn't even been thinking about getting married, but I got swept up in this whirlwind romance and his insistence that we were 'meant' to be together. He assured me he would plan everything, and I ended up giving in to his intensity.

"And he did plan everything. He planned the wedding, our honeymoon, our home . . . and the next five years of my life. The night before we were supposed to walk down the aisle, I had a heart-to-heart with my sister and maid of honor. In the middle of our celebratory evening my sister looked at me and asked, 'What's wrong?' I started crying and confessed, 'I want to get in a car, start driving, and never look back.'

"Stunned, she asked, 'Why?' I admitted I didn't want to marry my husband-to-be. He had given me the bum's rush (if only I'd realized then how true those words would be) and I had said yes because he'd had more than enough conviction for both of us. My gut was telling me not to go through with the wedding, but I thought it was too late to back out."

Are You Dealing with a Control-Monger?

I'm in favor of free expression, provided it's kept rigidly in control.
—ALAN BENNETT, BRITISH ACTOR

"Over the next few years, as long as I went along with what Ron wanted, things were okay. When I started getting a mind of my own, life started going downhill fast. If I didn't want to do what he wanted, when he wanted, the way he wanted, he got upset. If I questioned his opinion about something, there was hell to pay. I went to a therapist to get some advice, and after listening to me for a while, she asked, 'Why did you marry such a controlling person?'

"I laughed in instant recognition of the truth. 'It never even occurred to me that he was controlling,' I told her, shaking my head. 'I just thought he really loved me.' The therapist told me that Ron had displayed the classic signs of a controlling bully early on, I just hadn't known it. The urgent pursuit, the pressure to commit, the handling of all the details—all were indications of someone who has to be in charge.

"In retrospect, there were other danger signs; I just didn't recognize them. In that first year, he started to cut me off from the people I cared about. He never wanted to go to my folks' house for Sunday dinner and he was always trashing my friends. When I met him, he was really unhappy with his job and very bitter about his ex-wife. I just thought he had a bad boss and a witch for an ex-wife. It was only after being around him a while that I realized *every* manager he worked with was incompetent and *every* woman in his life had somehow 'screwed him over.' I wish I had listened to my intuition. When he was telling me all these terrible things about his former wife, this little voice inside me said, 'Someday he's going to be saying those kinds of things about you.' That little voice was right."

Beware: Bullies in the Area

> A person who is nice to you, but rude to the waiter,
> is not a nice person.
> —DAVE BARRY

This man had indeed displayed several of the ominous characteristics of a control freak. One of the primary signs was that he hurried her into getting hitched. He was afraid she'd "find him out" if he waited too long, so he rushed her to the altar before she had time to discover what he was really like.

If you're getting involved with someone, you might want to compare his/her behavior to the following checklist to see how he or she stacks up. In addition to the behaviors we've already discussed (ignoring or violating other people's rights, incessant demands and demeans), these behaviors are a red flag that something's amiss with this individual. If you observe more than a few of these characteristics, you might want to bide your time and get to know this person better before making any long-term commitment.

Checklist of Telltale Traits of a Tyrant

1. **DISSONANCE.** Psychologists agree that one of the primary indicators of a troubled person is incongruent behavior. As Dave Barry pointed out, someone who is nice to you and nasty to "the help" is not who he or she seems. Someone

who lets slip racist remarks and then tries to laugh them off is revealing his or her true character (or lack of it). Someone who says he or she loves children but seems remote or rigid when around them is displaying dissonance—defined as "inconsistency between the beliefs one holds and his or her actions." What this means is that you cannot take this person at his or her word. Everything they say will be suspect because you won't know when they're telling the truth and when they're not.

2. **POSSESSIVENESS.** Someone who comes on strong and wants (or has!) to be with you constantly is showing a dangerous need to have you all to him or herself. Possessiveness is defined as "a desire to own or dominate." Bullies often don't have many (or any) friends of their own, which means they grow to resent your other relationships. Does this person pout or try to make you feel guilty for abandoning him or her when you spend time with others? Does this person want to know all about your previous partners, and somehow resent the fact that you've been with someone other than him or her? Bullies are so insecure they see everyone you care for as competition and as a threat to their dominance. This reluctance to share you with others will only get worse and become more perverse.

3. **SECRECY.** People who don't want to discuss where they work and live and don't want you to meet their friends or family may have something to hide. People who refuse to reveal anything about their past are often concealing emotional baggage. What you don't know can hurt you. Someone who doles out self-revelations in small quantities may seem mysterious and alluring in the beginning. In the long run, being with a private person who withholds most of himself or herself gets lonesome.

4. **BITTERNESS.** Does this person have a lot of animosity toward his or her parents, former spouse, or previous managers? Please understand you will be reliving and working out the unresolved traumas of this individual's childhood and prior relationships. You've heard the Zen saying "Wherever you go, there you are"? This person hasn't yet figured out that his or her source of enmity is internal, not external. If this individual is lugging around deep-seated resentments or bitterness, it is only a matter of time before he or she starts accusing you of the same "crimes" former significant others supposedly perpetrated upon him or her.

5. **CRUELTY TO DOMESTIC ANIMALS.** It's one thing to dislike dogs or be allergic to cats. It's quite another to intentionally injure an innocent animal. People who see no harm in deliberately wounding a living creature lack humanity. If you see someone purposely inflict pain on an animal, don't accept any explanations. Head for the nearest exit. The next animal they hurt may be you. (Please note that hunters can be exempt from this. In certain areas, hunting is still a tradition and doesn't necessarily connote a unmerciful spirit. Draw your own conclusions about the potential of cruelty based on this individual's treatment of all animals.)

6. **TWISTS WORDS.** Does this person take what you say and turn it into something you didn't mean? Do you sometimes feel on the defensive and don't even know why? Does this person obfuscate—make confusing statements and then accuse you of misunderstanding? Bullies often make and break promises and then claim they never made them in the first place. This is a crazy-making ploy designed to turn you inside out so you don't know what's up.

7. HOLDS YOU RESPONSIBLE FOR THEIR UNHAPPINESS. Does this person blame you for his or her bad moods? If he's sad, it's because you didn't ask about his day? If she's depressed, it's because you don't take her anywhere anymore? If he's angry, it's because you said something that provoked him? There will be no pleasing this kind of person. Such people essentially haven't grown up, and never will as long as they hold everyone else but themselves accountable for how they feel.

8. PERFECTIONIST. Does this person nitpick? Does he or she have such high standards no one ever measures up? Does this individual have to do things himself because anyone else would just "mess it up"? If you're still in the honeymoon or courting phase, you may be temporarily exempt from this person's unceasing criticism. In time, though, his or her insistence on things being done a certain way (his or her way) will transfer to you, and then you'll never be able to do anything right. Jimmy Hoffa once said, "I may have my faults, but being wrong isn't one of them." Tyrants won't admit to *any* faults, least of all being wrong.

9. PINPOINTS YOUR WEAKNESS AND USES IT AGAINST YOU. Tyrants have a talent for ferreting out your emotional Achilles' heel and using it as ammunition. If you don't want to be considered selfish, they'll call you selfish. If you don't want to be perceived as controlling, they'll accuse you of being controlling. If you're unsure of your parenting skills, they'll attack your parenting skills. This is a classical Machiavellian method of exploiting your weakness so you're impotent (lacking power or strength) and they're omnipotent (having unlimited influence or authority). Their goal is to make you doubt yourself so you're vulnerable to their attempts to own you.

10. **PLAYS THE MARTYR.** Does he or she try to lay on the guilt trip by saying things like "Go ahead and go skiing with your friends. I don't mind. I mean, who wants to spend time with an old fogie like me anyway? I'm sure I'll find something to do." Does this person play the long-suffering individual who's unappreciated? Is it a common theme that he or she is the only one who holds things together and everyone else is frivolous and hedonistic, thinking only of him or herself?

11. **HATES TO HAVE HIS OR HER AUTHORITY QUESTIONED.** Does this person take umbrage if you dare dispute his or her facts, opinions, or observations? Does he or she come across as a know-it-all who has to have all the answers? Bullies can't stand to be challenged because they're afraid their "powerhouse of cards" could come falling down. Their "my way or the highway" communication style is based on their need to be in control and beyond reproach.

    If you disagree with this person, does he or she escalate their intensity in an effort to force you to concede? If so, this means that every conversation is going to turn into a verbal battleground. It means this person will start disparaging your intelligence, expertise, and experience so you no longer have the confidence or strength to challenge him or her.

12. **LIES, LIES, LIES.** Mark Twain once commented that "Truth is more of a stranger than fiction." Does that description fit the person you're dealing with? Does he or she self-aggrandize and exaggerate his or her achievements? In order to win respect, bullies often claim to have visited places they've never been, know people they've never met, and excel at things they've never tried.

    In the mid-1970s, I had the privilege of working with

Grand Slam tennis champion Rod Laver at his Hilton Head Island resort. A couple of times a year we sponsored national tennis camps. Every once in a while, someone would blow in the pro shop at the beginning of a new camp, and we would sense that we were about to deal with a type of individual the Aussies playfully refer to as "all flap and no throttle." These blowhards always talked a bigger game than they delivered.

Does the person you're dealing with display blowhard tendencies? Does he or she wax eloquent (or not so eloquent) about past accomplishments? Did this individual somehow manage in the first few minutes of meeting you to let you know how much money he made, what degrees she had, or what awards he's won? Was she so intent on impressing you with her curriculum vitae that she failed to ask about yours? Watch out. Red alert. Bellicose bully on the loose.

Way 8, "Respond to the Strategy, Not the Substance," shared some "Do the You" ways to cut off these "whatever gloats your boat" types. For now, what's important is to understand that these "look at me" personality types *don't change*. What you see and hear is what you'll get . . . and get and get.

Beware of the "Fault" Line

> My mother could make anyone feel guilty. She used to get
> letters of apology from people she didn't even know.
> —JOAN RIVERS

A man named Steve talked to me following a seminar. He said, "I think anyone getting into a relationship ought to read through this checklist first. It sent chills up and down my spine because you described my ex-girlfriend to a T. She displayed every single one of those characteristics. She chased me until she caught me; then once she caught me, I couldn't do anything right. She used to listen in on my phone calls and interrogate me about my old girlfriends. She was paranoid about me even looking at another woman. She smothered me. What's worse is that somehow she made me feel that everything was my fault. Even when I tried to end the relationship, it was because '*I* was giving up on us' and '*I* was afraid of commitment.' She tried to make me feel guilty for 'throwing her out,' and for her having given up her apartment, even though she was the one who had pushed so hard to move in with me. She never for a moment considered that she played any role in what went wrong. It was all on me."

Are You Dealing with a Part-time or a Full-time Tyrant?

A critic is someone who's at his best when you're at your worst.
—TONY PELLETO

A tyrant is someone who does his or her best to make you feel worse. Are you involved with someone who displays a mixture of these traits? Are you thinking, "Well, my partner does some of these things some of the times, but so do I! After all, no one is perfect."

You're right. The key issue is how *frequently* your partner engages in these behaviors and whether he or she is willing to change. Do you have any clout or leverage with him or her? Is he or she open to input or would s/he dispute anything you say? Way 14, "Know When to Hold 'Em, When to Fold 'Em," has a series of questions you can ask to determine whether this relationship is worth saving or whether you may need to end the relationship to save yourself. First, it's important to evaluate whether one reason this individual has been taking advantage of your good nature is because you're too good-natured.

Action Plan and Discussion Questions

Think back to a bully you dealt with in your life. Did he or she display any telltale traits of a tyrant in the beginning? Which ones? _____

_____

_____

At the time, did you believe those behaviors were a temporary, legitimate result of negative situations? Explain. _____

_____

_____

Is there a person in your life right now who has more than five of these traits? Does knowing these are patterns of behaviors motivate you to change your relationship with this person? Why or why not? _____

_____

_____

Could you be contributing to this unsatisfactory relationship? What is your role in what's happening? _____

_____

_____

Summary

HARMFUL BELIEFS/BEHAVIORS	HELPFUL BELIEFS/BEHAVIORS
The tyrant takes control *"I want you to move in with me."*	You stay in control *"I prefer to stay in my own home."*
Dissonance *"My parents and I get along fine, but I haven't seen them for years."*	Congruence *"I love my folks and hope you'll enjoy meeting them."*
Possessiveness *"Why do you need your friends when you've got me?"*	Shares you with others *"Have a good time with your friends tonight."*
Secrecy *"I don't like to talk about that."*	An open book *"What do you want to know?"*
Bitter about unresolved issues *"I'll never forgive him for what he did to me."*	Has resolved issues *"I learned a lot from him and I'm better for it."*
Twists words *"I never said that. You must be making it up."*	Accountable for words *"You're right, I did agree to take care of that."*
Holds you responsible for his/her moods *"I'm depressed because you got the promotion I deserved."*	Is responsible for own moods *"I'm sad because I didn't get the promotion I wanted."*

Perfectionist	Attainable standards
"Can't you do anything right?"	*"Thanks for putting the dishes away."*
Uses your weakness against you	Doesn't exploit weakness
"You're going to turn out just like your mother— a dried-up old hag."	*"Honey, I think you look fine the way you are."*
Hates to have authority questioned	Doesn't have to have all the answers
"You don't know what you're saying."	*"That's a good point."*

Way 11. Police Your Puh-lease

Exaggerated sensitiveness is an expression of the
feeling of inferiority.
—ALFRED ADLER

A SINGLE LADY ASKED RATHER PLAINTIVELY, "I DON'T UNDERSTAND
it. I'm a nice person. Why is it the last three guys I've gone out
with all turned out to be jerks?"

The answer may surprise her and you. As Adler points out,
oversensitiveness can indicate an unhealthy overeagerness to
seek approval. Bullies actively seek out people pleasers because
they can count on them to continue going along to get along.

You may wonder, "What's the connection?" Pleasers often
come from unhappy homes in which they received limited
support or love. They thought being obedient and agreeable
was the way to get their parents' attention, so they did their best
to be the good little boy or girl. Even as adults, they continue
to try to ingratiate themselves to authority figures to get the
acceptance they never received as kids. Pleasers are approval
junkies. If someone doesn't like them, they quickly self-
examine to see if they did "something wrong" and adapt to get
back in the other person's good graces.

Is Everybody Happy?

The reward for conformity is that everyone likes you except
yourself.
—RITA MAE BROWN, AMERICAN WRITER

The pleasers' motto is "Is everybody happy?" They are quick
to see other people's points of view instead of their own, and
frequently give up their opinions with comments like "It
doesn't matter" or "I don't mind" when it does matter and
they do mind. They are the quintessential "No, you go first"
personality types. As a result, many pleasers feel put upon by
their family members, co-workers, and acquaintances. They
don't want to risk alienating anyone, so they say yes instead of
no even when they don't want to be in charge of the third
grade bake sale and they don't want to let their neighbor bor-
row their lawn mower—again.

As you can imagine, this takes a toll. Pleasers are so desperate
for harmony, they pay almost any price to keep the peace.
Unfortunately, that price is often the sacrifice of their "please
of mind." While outwardly, pleasers often appear to have it all
together, internally they feel taken advantage of. Not that
they'll complain about it. They wouldn't dare risk alienating
public affection. Only to themselves will they admit their
heartbreak because everyone seems to take their generosity for
granted.

Do You Have a Pleasing Personality?

You can please some of the people some of the time, and all of the
people some of the time, but some of the people you can't please
none of the time.
—TOM WILSON AS ZIGGY

Are you wondering, "What's this got to do with bullies?" Bullies partner with pleasers for several reasons. First, bullies are
often disliked and they want to feed off the popularity of their
well-liked partner. They're hoping that associating with a
charming mate will cause people to hold them in higher
regard.

Second, bullies are often obsessed with status. They want to
prove they're big shots, which is why they often have fancy
houses, expensive toys, and trophy spouses. It's a "look at me"
attempt to loom large in people's eyes and inspire envy.

Third, bullies are privately envious of pleasant personalities.
(Note the common origins of the word "pleasant" and
"please.") Harville Hendrix's groundbreaking research into
relationships says that we seek mates who complete us. We look
for qualities in our partner that we admire and that we lack.
Since many bullies lack social graces, they're consciously or
unconsciously hoping that their mate's social skills will rub off
on them and they'll acquire the characteristics they lack but
secretly long for.

Finally, tyrannical bullies know that pleasers will kowtow to
their domineering ways. The compulsive need to live in harmony that pleasers feel means they often end up acquiescing in
an effort to avoid unsettling conflict. Bullies know all they have
to do to get a pleaser to give in and give up is to get ugly. They
know pleasers will capitulate rather than risk the dreaded
unpleasantness.

So do you have a "pleasing" personality? If so, this otherwise attractive quality may have attracted the wrong kind of individuals—people who are more interested in exploiting your pleasantness than in appreciating it.

You Can't Appease All the People All the Time

An appeaser is one who feeds a crocodile—
hoping it will eat him last.
—SIR WINSTON CHURCHILL

"Boy, does this strike home," a man named Daniel said. "I was the only child of a distant and cold mother. Nothing I did was ever good enough. My childhood was a vain attempt to get her to notice me. So what did I do when it was time to get married? I found someone just like 'dear ole Mom,' of course.

"I tied myself in knots trying to make my wife happy. No matter how hard I tried, she always found something wrong with it or me. Sound familiar?" he asked, smiling at his own expense. "If I took her out for dinner for our anniversary, she wanted to know why I hadn't gotten her flowers. If I got a raise at work, she wanted to know why I hadn't gotten one sooner. If I bought her a dress, she wanted it in a different color. There was just no pleasing this woman." He laughed out loud at what he had just said.

Please (oops) note this man's insight. It is impossible to please some people. In particular, it is impossible to please tyrants because they don't want to be content, they want to be in control.

Efforts to cajole a bully will never work because a bully wants to perpetuate the cycle of his or her partner's never obtaining approval and therefore trying harder to win it. Why? The emotionally distant person in a relationship rules that relationship. By withholding what their partner wants, bullies keep control. Bullies adopt aloofness or aggressiveness as a way to keep pleasers on an emotional leash. Bullies are disapproving on purpose because they know appeasers abhor rejection and will renew their efforts to "keep the please."

Do You Like to Be Liked?

> How I like to be liked, and what I do to be liked!
> —CHARLES LAMB

The question is, how can we change what is, for some of us, a lifetime habit of relating to others? Next time you're about to say yes to a request or give in to a command—whether it's agreeing to cover for a co-worker while she takes a long lunch or going to see a violent movie you would rather not watch—take this questionnaire.

Who Am I Trying to Please and Why?

Am I doing this because . . .

1. I owe this person a favor and it's a fair exchange?
2. It's a tangible expression of my love or respect for this person?
3. They deserve what they're requesting?
4. It's a way to honor them or say thank-you?
5. It's a present for a special occasion?
6. It's my "job" and I'm required to?
7. I know in my heart it's the right thing to do?
8. I truly want to? I'm doing it willingly and without coercion.
9. I want to contribute to this person (or to mankind) in a positive way?

10. It will serve me and give me something I want (money, status, satisfaction, pleasure, more time)?
11. I'm trying to buy this person's approval?
12. I don't want this person to get mad at me?
13. I have a sense of obligation and feel I should say yes?
14. I don't know how to say no?
15. I don't want to hurt this person's feelings?
16. I'm afraid people will think less of me if I don't?
17. This person is pressuring me with "Everybody else does it"?
18. I'm afraid this person will cause a scene if I don't give in?
19. I habitually agree to do what people want?
20. I don't have the strength, clarity, or courage to not go along?

As you can probably see, answering yes to some of the first ten questions means you have valid reasons for granting this person's request. You are agreeing for all the right reasons. Answering yes to some of the next ten questions means you would be abdicating your own rights, needs, and desires; indeed, it is *not* in your best interest to give in to what this person wants. Saying yes because of the second group of reasons indicates a serious case of the disease to please.

Four Steps to "No" Power

> Do you have "No" power or do you have no power?
> —SONYA FRIEDMAN

The path to power requires learning how to respectfully refuse people's unreasonable requests. If being agreeable has become a habit, you can begin reversing it by resolving to take these four steps to "No" power. From now on, when people ask you to do something, vow to:

1. **TAKE TIME TO MAKE YOUR DECISION.** A friend has a coffee mug that says, "Patience comes to those who wait." Well, wiser decisions come to those who wait. Say, "I want a few moments to think this over." If the other person tries to pressure you, simply say, "Fine, if you have to have an answer right now, it's no." Then get away from this person so you can think this through in private. Delaying your answer and removing yourself from their sphere of influence prevents bullies from mentally crowding you. You are literally and figuratively giving yourself some space so you can get perspective on this issue and determine whether saying yes is in your best interests.

2. **REVIEW THIS PERSON'S RIGHTS/NEEDS SEESAW HISTORY.** Has this person consistently been over the top with demands and demeans? Have you been a "guilt sponge" and absorbed more than your fair share of the responsibility for making this relationship work? Think about whether you've been consistently giving up what you want and this person has been getting almost all of what he or she wants.

3. **DETERMINE IF SAYING NO IS WHAT'S REQUIRED TO KEEP A BALANCE OF POWER.** Understand it's your responsibility (not the other person's) to make sure your needs are met, your rights are respected, and your desires are granted. If saying yes will perpetuate a "one up one down" relationship— with you on the bottom—it's time to refuse this request so the relationship will be more equitable.

4. **KEEP IT BRIEF OR THEY'LL GIVE YOU GRIEF.** The more succinct you are, the more convincing you'll be. Do not offer long-winded explanations. The more reasons you give for your decision, the more ammunition you give aggressive individuals to shoot down your answer. The more you hedge, the harder they'll press.

Don't Get Drawn Into Debating Your Position

> It is easier to stay out than to get out.
> —MARK TWAIN

Anticipate that manipulators will try to make you feel bad for not giving them what they want. If, for example, a co-worker says, "But you've always covered for me before," simply repeat what you said and do not get drawn into defending your decision. As Twain observed, it is easier to stay out than get out of an argument. If you try to justify your refusal by saying, "Well, I have too much to do today," a habitual exploiter will quickly say, "Well, I'll only be gone an hour." If we weakly protest, "Explosion-a-minute movies make me uncomfortable," a controlling person will sense our ambivalence and pile on extra pressure: "Come on. It got good reviews. Do it for me."

Explaining to bullies why we don't want to do what they want leads to debates. It's better simply to refuse over-the-top requests without justifying ourselves. Keep the responsibility ball in their court by saying, "You'll have to find someone else" or "I'm not going to see violent movies anymore. Period."

You can also say, "My mind's made up" or "This is non-negotiable." They may stomp off, but remember, you are no longer going to try to please everyone at your own expense. You don't have to be mean, just mean what you say. From now on, reverse the "disease to please" by:

- Understanding the unhealthy pathology behind needing everyone's approval
- Recognizing it's right to balance your needs and wants with those of others instead of constantly giving in to others' needs and wants

- Asking the "Who Am I Trying to Please and Why?" questions to determine if you're agreeing to this person's request for the right reasons
- Firmly refusing over-the-line requests without defending your rationale
- Becoming clear that you want "No" power instead of no power
- Remembering that in the final analysis, what matters is whether *you* approve of what you do and how you behave

Are You Too Nice for Your Own Good?

Why is it moral to serve the happiness of others and not your own?
—Ayn Rand, *Atlas Shrugged*

The moral of this chapter is that happiness is best achieved by serving yourself in balance with serving others. Being nice should not require the sacrifice of your rights and needs. Being clear about this is central to having the assurance to not give in to intimidating tactics. The next chapter explains how we can turn doubt into clout so bullies can see at a glance that we're not too nice for our own good.

Action Plan and Discussion Questions

Are you a people pleaser? If so, what do you think contributed to you becoming one? _____

_____

_____

_____

Do you mostly seek approval from men or women, peers or authority figures? Explain. _____
_____
_____

What's a relationship with a significant other in which you traditionally go along to keep the please? Who is that person? What are some ways you try to win approval or keep harmony? _____
_____
_____

How has this affected you? What are some of the consequences you've paid to be liked? _____
_____
_____

Have you recently agreed to a favor even though you didn't want to? Talk yourself through the "Who Am I Trying to Please and Why?" questionnaire. Why did you say yes? _____
_____
_____

Are you being pressured right now to do something? What steps are you going to take to produce an answer that honors your rights and needs, not just the other person's? _____
_____
_____

If you decide to have "No" power, how are you going to refuse another's request without weakening under his or her pressure? _____
_____
_____

Summary

HARMFUL BELIEFS/BEHAVIORS	HELPFUL BELIEFS/BEHAVIORS
Pleaser who gives in and goes along to get approval *"Okay, we'll go to the war museums while we're in Paris."*	Person who balances own rights and needs with those of others *"I know you want to go to the museum, and I want to see the French Open."*
Caring about whether we're liked means our self-respect is in other people's hands *Thinking, "If I don't give in, he'll pout and make both of us miserable."*	Caring about what's fair means our self-respect is in our hands *"I have the right to do what I want on our vacation, too."*
Automatically saying yes because we want to "keep the please" *"No, it's okay, really. I'm sure I'll learn a lot."*	Asking the "Who Am I Trying to Please and Why?" questions *"I want to take a few minutes to think this over."*
No power and no self-worth *"I can't believe we came all this way and I'll miss seeing Andre Agassi play."*	"No" power builds self-worth *"I've got a plan. You go to the museum and I'll go to the tournament."*
Explain your rationale *"I don't think it's fair that we always have to do what you want."*	Keep your brief short *"We'll meet back at the hotel tonight and swap our adventures."*

Way 12. Realize Clarity Rules

> I had nothing to offer anybody except my own confusion.
> —JACK KEROUAC

CLARITY IS *THE* KEY TO HAVING THE CONFIDENCE TO CONFRONT bullies. Why? Confusion immobilizes. When we're not sure what we believe, we're not sure what to say or do, and when we don't know what to say or do, we usually don't say or do anything. Bullies capitalize on this uncertainty to press their advantage.

At one point in my battle with a bully, the tactics being used against me were unconscionable. I was considering giving in just to get it over with. I was also in the midst of writing this book and was spending every spare minute working on it. I was flying to Toronto on a puddle jumper to present a Tongue Fu! seminar, and was working on this chapter while wondering what action to take or not take. All of a sudden, my brain was on fire and the "Clarity Rules" poured out of my mind so fast my fingers could hardly keep up. I will be forever grateful for that divine guidance or whatever it was.

I hope these rules give you the willpower they've given me.

Clarity produces conviction. Conviction keeps us strong. Think about it: If you're clear that your children are your top priority, it's easier to say no to going out with the gang after work, because you know you want to get to the field on time to watch your son's soccer game. When we are clear that we have a right to be treated with respect, we don't allow people to treat us with disrespect.

Believe in Your Bill of Rights

Who do I think I am, anyway?
—GRAFFITO

Imprint the following "Clarity Rules" in your mind. Believe them in your gut. Post them where you can see them throughout the day. Carry a copy in your wallet so you can pull them out when the occasion warrants. Review them frequently for a shot of courage. The clearer we are about who we are, the less vulnerable we'll be to a bully's effort to railroad us.

Start Your Own Emancipation Project

The five most dangerous words in the English language:
"Maybe it will go away."
—SIGN IN DENTIST'S OFFICE

Many of us studied the Declaration of Independence and the Emancipation Proclamation in school. Yet some of us along the way lost our belief that we each have inalienable human rights. For whatever reason, we gave up control of our lives to someone who sought power over us.

Emancipation is defined as "to free from restraint, control, bondage, or the power of another." Our goal is to develop and

Clarity Rules

- I have clarity that my definition of a healthy relationship is one in which I have the freedom to think and act for myself.

- I have clarity that I choose to believe the best of people, and I give them the benefit of the doubt until they prove me wrong.

- I have clarity that I will be kind and compassionate until someone tries to take advantage of my good nature.

- I have clarity that I will seek win-win resolutions until it is obvious the other person refuses to play by the rules.

- I have clarity that it is my responsibility to speak up if someone crosses the line of common decency.

- I have clarity that suffering in silence perpetuates the problem.

- I have clarity that I will speak up if someone tries to intimidate me.

- I have clarity that I will walk tall so bullies won't perceive I'm weak.

- I have clarity that I am a worthwhile person who has the right to stand up for my needs if someone tries to trample them.

- I have clarity that I will ask myself, "What's my culpability?" so that I do not unwittingly contribute to or perpetuate a bully's mistreatment of me.

- I have clarity that I will set and state limits in advance so people know my boundaries and ethical threshold.

- I have clarity that I will no longer "keep the please" at any price.

- I have clarity that I want to serve as a role model for my loved ones that we do not passively endure someone verbally abusing us.

- I have clarity that I will not volunteer to be a victim, and I will remove myself from a relationship in which someone is trying to control or own me.

- I have clarity that words can hurt and haunt. I will not demean others and I will not allow anyone to demean me or a loved one.

- I have clarity that life is a blessing, not a burden, and I will not allow bullies to undermine my sanity or that of my loved ones.

- I have clarity that I am responsible for my physical and mental health, and I take appropriate action to improve unsafe situations.

- I have clarity that I do not give myself up and I do not give up on myself.

adopt our own personal Bill of Rights so we can emancipate ourselves from the individuals who have been bullying us. Understand that bullies will not just go away and voluntarily leave us alone. Why should they? They've got a good thing going. We must take responsibility for ending a dominant/doormat situation or it will continue.

Confusion Buries the Way

> What impresses me about America is how well parents
> obey their children.
> —DUKE OF WINDSOR

Remember earlier in the book we clarified that bullies come in all shapes, sizes, and ages? These "Clarity Rules" apply to our relationships with children as well. As the Duke of Windsor observed, some adults answer to their children instead of the other way around.

"Talk about confused," Abigail commented. "My twenty-two-year-old daughter had me turned inside out and upside down. I was supposed to be the parent in the relationship, but she had me twisted around her little finger.

"I had always dreamed of those close mother-daughter relationships where you went shopping together, swapped clothes, and shared confidences. It was never like that with us. Tiffany's teen years were a nightmare. She stayed out past curfew, had terrible grades, and stole money from my purse. My friends told me her disobedience was typical adolescence and she would grow out of it. She never did.

"Tiffany came home after college because she couldn't find work. A couple of months stretched into six months, six months stretched into a year, and she still hadn't found the 'right' job. During this time, she was wrecking my town house, when she wasn't lying around watching soaps. Every time I tried to talk to her, she'd turn things around and say I was unsympathetic.

"I tried to get her to go to therapy with me, but she wouldn't. I finally went myself. The therapist sat through that entire first session and hardly spoke. She just let me pour out my frustration. Over the next few weeks, she helped me see that I was being bullied by my own daughter and that I had enabled this situation by not setting and enforcing ground rules. She helped me understand that the way out of this mess was to keep asking myself, 'Who's the parent?' and by giving Tiffany what she needed rather than what she wanted. She also suggested I pull a mea culpa."

Mea Culpa, Mea Culpa

When a man points a finger at someone else, he should remember
that four of his fingers are pointing at himself.
—Louis Nizer

Abigail continued. "Mea culpa is Latin for 'my fault.' The therapist told me trying to rein Tiffany in at this point was going to be tough because the precedent was set that she could do whatever she pleased. The only way to change this losing game was for me to take responsibility for letting things get out of hand. After all, Tiffany was only doing what I had let her get away with. The therapist helped me write up 'House Rules' and told me how to resurrect a more proper parent-child relationship.

"The following Monday, I told Tiffany we were going to have the first of what was going to become a weekly family meeting. The therapist had emphasized how important it was to make this a formal ritual rather than a casual get-together, so we sat down at the dining room table. I explained it was my fault things had gotten out of hand, that I realized the error of my ways, and that things were going to be different from now on."

Permissiveness Promotes Pandemonium

> Pandemonium didn't reign, it poured.
> —JOHN K. BANGS

"I laid out the house rules and explained that as an adult, if she wanted to continue living in our home, she needed to obey the rules because we were no longer going to live in pandemonium. I explained that family members living together agree to abide by common laws of decency so everyone can coexist cooperatively. I explained that every family member (even if there are just two of us) needs to contribute so household maintenance and upkeep are kept equitable. I explained that if family members choose to ignore these rules or abuse the rights of housemates, they lose their right to live in that home.

"Tiffany just sat there, stunned. I told her I should have done this a long time ago, but had not been clear about my role as a parent. I now realized my job was to teach my child how to be a self-sufficient citizen who gets along in the world with others. I hadn't done her or me any favors by being so lax in my standards. I told her it wasn't too late for both of us to learn this lesson, and that I was going to hold us both accountable for behaving responsibly.

"Some of our house rules included basic rules of courtesy. Not calling each other names. Calling by six P.M. to say whether you're going to be home in time for dinner. Cleaning up messes in common areas—the same day! Divvying up household chores. This is where I asked for her input. We made up a list of what needed to be done and went through the list, alternating choices.

"I also told Tiffany, 'A condition of you continuing to live here is that we go to counseling together once a week. If you have issues with this, we can work them out with the therapist.' I wrapped up by saying, 'I have absolute clarity about this, and there will be no wavering or giving in to pressure or excuses. If you break the rules once, you get a warning. If you break them again, you'll need to get your own apartment and support yourself, and no amount of begging, pleading, or name-calling will get me to change my mind.' I told her I was looking forward to living together in harmony, and I hoped this would be one of the best things that ever happened to us. It was."

A woman who heard this story asked skeptically, "Do you really think that a mother would have thrown her daughter out of the house?" I told her, "She needed to be prepared to do just that or otherwise she'd be a paper tiger. Empty threats serve no one. That's why it's so important to be clear about the appropriateness of your proposed action. The mother was doing the right thing by claiming culpability for the past and by outlining the new policies and consequences for the future. If the daughter chose to break the rules, it would be *her* fault she's out of house and home, not her mother's. 'Tough love' is simply a way of teaching people that they will be held accountable for their behavior, whether they like it or not. Instead of the world revolving around them, they learn that if they do the crime, they pay big-time."

Things Are Going to Be Different from Now On

> You might as well fall flat on your face as
> lean over too far backwards.
> —JAMES THURBER

Are you in an untenable situation right now? Have you given yourself a bad back by bending over backward to accommodate someone who is breaking the rules? Has your confusion about your role or rights perpetuated this problem? Is it time to draw up your own Rules of the Woed (as one seminar pundit named them)?

Remember to pull a mea culpa so the people affected don't

feel they're being unfairly blamed for behavior they were never held accountable for in the first place. That's the catch-22 of not explaining and enforcing policies up front. Rule breakers may initially know what they're doing is wrong, but if no one complains, they conclude that it must not be that bad. Their logic is "If it was really important, you'd stop me, so I guess this must be okay."

Fresh Start

> I worry incessantly that I might be too clear.
> —ALAN GREENSPAN

You don't need to worry about being too clear. It's when people aren't clear that problems begin. When people know exactly what's accepted and what's not, crossing the line is kept to a minimum.

You may even want to use a phrase my son learned at Montessori to indicate that misbehavior someone used to get away with will no longer be tolerated. Five-year-old Andrew had been given a time-out after I discovered his colorful mural on our hall wall. After an hour in his room, Andrew came out, shuffled his feet on the floor, looked up at me, and asked hopefully, "Fresh start?"

Those two words have become our way to indicate that the past is past so we don't carry grudges. If something has gone wrong, we make apologies or amends, and then actually clap our hands together so we can close the books on the subject and have a clean transition. Sometimes I even point over my shoulder and say something like "That's behind us now." You may even want to pretend you're erasing an imaginary chalkboard while saying "Let's wipe the slate clean." This may seem contrived, but your gestures will reinforce what you're saying and make your abstract words more concrete.

You can have a fresh start even if you and a loved one turned bully have had a bad start. Establish your own Rules of the Woed. Post them where everyone can see them. Claim mea culpa if appropriate. Tell someone who's been breaking the rules such inappropriate behavior is a thing of the past. Agree to a fresh start and move forward with assurance that things are going to be different from now on.

Action Plan and Discussion Questions

Did anyone ever teach you that you had rights? If so, who was that person and how did he or she tell you this? _____

_____

_____

_____

Do you agree with the rights in the "Clarity Rules"? Are there any you would like to edit or add? Which ones? _____

_____

_____

_____

Are you in a situation that's overdue for some rules? What are they and how are you going to establish them? _____

_____

_____

_____

Visualize meeting with this person. What exactly are you going to say to claim mea culpa and agree to a fresh start?

_____

_____

_____

How are you going to let him or her know that things are
going to be different from now on? _____
_____
_____

Summary

HARMFUL BELIEFS/BEHAVIORS	HELPFUL BELIEFS/BEHAVIORS
Confusion immobilizes *"He's not that bad a person.* *He's got some good qualities."*	Clarity aids action *"Calling me names is* *inexcusable."*
No rules, so anything goes *"He had a lot of nerve accusing* *me of flirting with our neighbor* *in front of everyone."*	Rules of the Woed *"Harry, do you remember* *we agreed not to snipe* *at each other in public?"*
Bullies own us and we answer to them *"He won't give me my allowance* *if I make him mad, though."*	We adopt our own Bill of Rights *"Harry, I don't let anyone* *verbally abuse me."*
Claim it's the other person's fault *"What do you mean, you* *wouldn't do it if I wasn't* *asking for it?"*	Claim mea culpa *"Perhaps I didn't make it* *clear how I feel about this."*
Things never change *"He's doing it again!"*	Things are different from now on *"Don't do this again."*

Way 13. Put Up a Brave Front

It is never too late to do right.
—Ralph Waldo Emerson

ONE OF THE BEST WAYS TO DO RIGHT BY YOURSELF IS TO LITERALLY and figuratively *stand up* for yourself. Bullies assess our clarity of purpose and our confidence (or lack of) by our body language.

This may sound like a blazing attack of the obvious, but bullies usually pick on people smaller than them. Have you noticed that the difficult people in your life often launch their verbal assaults when you're seated? Why is that? It's easier for them to tower over someone who's lower than them. They are trying to take physical advantage of their dominant position to reinforce their superiority and our inferiority.

An engineer named Matt chuckled upon hearing this and commented, "This reminds me of a co-worker at my previous job. He was rather short and compensated for it by swaggering around talking about the days when he had been in charge of this or that as a senior military officer. He was quick to point out your errors so he could correct them. One afternoon I was working on a set of blueprints and he came over and started pounding on my desk with his fist. He was upset because he'd just found out our project had some cost overruns. I wasn't going to sit there and take that because I knew the unapproved spending had been done by a different department.

"I stood up (I'm six-four) and started walking around my desk toward him. I was going to tell him he should get his facts straight, but I didn't have to. As I rounded the desk, he took off, muttering something under his breath."

Stand Up for Yourself

If you won't leave me alone, I'll find someone who will.
—COFFEE MUG SLOGAN

What Matt must have known at some intuitive level is that rising to our feet is a nonverbal way of saying "I'm not taking this sitting down." Staying seated actually encourages tyrannical behavior because it gives controllers the upper hand and keeps us under their thumb. When we stand up, we are no longer beneath them. In fact, the taller you can make yourself, the less likely a bully will feel he or she can lord over you and the more likely he or she will decide they have better things to do elsewhere.

I had the privilege of playing in a golf tournament with Mariah Burton-Nelson, a former professional basketball player and the author of *The Stronger Women Get, The More Men Like Football*. While waiting to tee off, I asked if she had any bully stories. She thought about it for a moment and then looked at me, mildly perplexed. "I can't think of any," she said. Of course not. Mariah is over six feet tall and is a confident, athletic woman who knows who she is. She simply is not bully material. One look at her sense of assurance and any bully would wisely leave her alone.

Don't Kowtow to Bullies

Bullies are always to be found where there are cowards.
—MAHATMA GANDHI

A friend pointed out, "I'm feeling some short-ism coming on here. Mariah has an unfair advantage. She's over six feet. I'm barely over five." Good point. There are still things you can do to appear tall even if you're not. Petite people can be perceived as powerful and can prevent would-be intimidators from invading their space as long as they project confidence.

Criminals have revealed that they seek out marks who have what they call a victim's stance. Victims walk or sit slightly hunched over. Victims often keep their chin down and their eyes averted or unfocused. They often hold their arms close to their body in a protective pose. They walk with small, hesitant steps or wander mindlessly. Unfortunately, this cowardly-appearing posture attracts bullies.

Confident people don't cower, they tower. They stand straight with their shoulders back. Their chest is out instead of concave. They keep their chin up and look at the world straight on with a calm, steady gaze. They walk purposefully and energetically. Even when in a chair, they sit up and project authority instead of slouching. Their whole demeanor says, "I know and like who I am."

A popular teen magazine interviewed me for an article on confidence. My first suggestion to young female readers was to stop hunching over and hugging their schoolbooks to their chest. This posture rolls their shoulders forward and makes them appear awkward and vulnerable. It's better to lug heavy textbooks in a backpack so they can walk tall with shoulders back, chin lifted, and strong, purposeful strides.

If you have a bully in your life right now, ask yourself what signals your body has been sending. Have you been feeling defeated? Has your posture reflected and reinforced that image? Do you slump when you're with this person? Do you give away your nervousness by flinching or leaning away? Do you keep your head down in the hopes he or she won't notice you? (Note: It didn't work with your third grade teacher and it won't work with a bully either.)

Mind Your Body

> After thirty, a body has a mind of its own.
> —BETTE MIDLER

A former security guard named Harold told me, "We need to keep in mind that bullies operate from a primal point of view. They measure their worth by where they are on the 'authority ladder' compared to the people around them. Life is one big pecking order for them. You're either higher in the hierarchy or lower. Bullies check out our body language in the first few seconds. If they perceive we're the 'bigger dog,' they'll usually leave us alone. If we indicate any hesitancy, they'll pounce. That's why it's so important to send the right signals. I train all my security personnel how to have a commanding presence. They can prevent a lot of fights just by the way they hold themselves."

Read again what Harold said: "They can prevent a lot of fights just by the way they hold themselves." Think about it. "You've got me in your hold" means you've got me in your clutches, in your control. Ergo, holding a powerful posture means we're controlling ourselves, which means the bully won't be able to.

More Power to You

Don't just do something; stand there.
—GEORGE P. SHULTZ

How do we hold a powerful posture? By putting up a brave front. One woman protested, "But I don't feel brave. How can I act brave?" Good question and good news. As discussed in my book *What's Holding You Back?: Thirty Days to Having the Confidence and Courage to Do What You Want, Go Where You Want, and Meet Whom You Want*, you can act courageous even if you don't feel courageous.

Most of us let our body reflect how we feel. From now on, use your body to direct how you feel. Psychologist William James said one of the most important discoveries he made in fifty years of studying human behavior was that it is easier to act ourselves into feeling than it is to feel ourselves into acting. In other words, if we wait until we feel strong to act strong, we may be waiting a *long* time. Our goal is to learn how to project confidence—even though we may not initially feel confident.

How do we do that? By minding our body and intentionally adopting a posture that exudes authority instead of allowing ourselves to appear weak and meek. Our brain is going to tell our body how to act, instead of our body telling our brain how to feel.

In the chart that follows, notice that the body positions on the left are usually a result of feeling frightened or intimidated. Notice that the body positions on the right can be held even if we are feeling afraid and intimidated—and the very act of assuming these postures increases our feeling of confidence.

What Signals Is Your Body Sending?

WEAK AND MEEK	AURA OF AUTHORITY
Head down	Head up
Chin tucked in	Chin out
Face averted	Face forward
Eyes darting	Eyes wide open
Look away	Look at
Shoulders slumped	Shoulders back
Chest caved in	Chest out
Legs crossed, close together	Legs apart, in ready position
Stand "hip shot"	Stand on two feet
Walk with hesitant steps	Walk with strong strides
Sit slouched	Sit straight
Lean away	Lean toward
Step back	Step up

Exude an Aura of Authority

YIELD (But Do Not Snivel)
—ROAD SIGN IN *ZIGGY* CARTOON BY TOM WILSON

It's been fascinating developing this chapter because of the dual significance of the phrases associated with authoritative body language. Standing on our own two feet means just that. It shows we're standing our ground instead of giving in to the flight urge and being poised to flee. Having our eyes wide open means we see what's in front of us instead of turning a blind eye toward the problem. Meeting a situation head-on means we're prepared to face it instead of looking for a way out. Stepping up to the plate (or the person) indicates a confident willingness to engage and is the opposite of backing down.

"I've heard about the importance of body language before," one skeptic commented. "I never thought of it this way, though—that I can regulate both how I feel and how other people feel about me by regulating my posture. It makes a lot of sense. I may not be able to control my emotions, but I can control the way I stand, sit, and walk. And by choosing to adopt a strong stance, I'll feel stronger and be perceived as stronger."

Pretend to Be a Tower of Power

> I pretended to be somebody I wanted to be until finally
> I became that person. Or he became me.
> —CARY GRANT

If you're near a mirror right now, take a minute to walk over and assume the "aura of authority" position. See for yourself how much more assured you look when you stand straight, square your shoulders and hold your head up. See how tentative you look when you duck your chin, allowing your shoulders to droop and your chest to cave in.

Remember, you can pretend to be brave even if you don't initially feel brave. By adopting the "tower of power" position, you will be perceived as being sure of yourself. People who are sure of themselves reverse the risk–reward ratio. Your brave front causes would-be attackers to take one look at you and decide, "I don't think so. This one would be too hard to handle."

Action Plan and Discussion Questions

Think about your customary body language. What signals do you send? Do you exude assurance or do you come across as weak and meek? Explain. _____

_____

_____

Do you have a bully in your life? If so, how does your body language change around this person? Do you cower or cringe? Give an example. _____

_____

_____

From now on, how are you going to project an aura of authority that says "I know who I am, don't mess with me" so bullies looking for an easy mark pass you by? _____

_____

_____

Summary

HARMFUL BELIEFS/BEHAVIORS	HELPFUL BELIEFS/BEHAVIORS
Take abuse sitting down *"I hate it when Paul comes into my office and launches into these tirades."*	Stand up to abuse *"Paul, did you have some helpful suggestions?"*

Appear meek and weak
*"I wish I could disappear.
When is he going to stop?"*

Exude aura of authority
*Walking toward him, "What
recommendations do you have?"*

Body language reflects
feelings
*"He makes me feel like
I'm about two inches tall."*

Body language directs feelings
*Putting shoulders back and looking
him in eye, "And what did
you like about that project?"*

Cower
*"Maybe if I just wait him out,
he'll get the hint."*

Tower
*I'm not going to take this sitting
down. Standing up, "Paul, that's
enough."*

Way 14. Know When to Hold 'Em, When to Fold 'Em

It's my rule never to lose my temper till it would be
detrimental to keep it.
—SEAN O'CASEY

WE'VE TALKED ABOUT BEING BRAVE, ABOUT BEING POSITIVELY
intolerant, and about beating 'em to the punch . . . line. Now
it's time to understand that it's not always smart to confront
someone whose behavior is objectionable. There are times
when it is detrimental to force the issue.

This insight emerged during an all-day Tongue Fu! program
for school administrators. The audience had been divided into
smaller groups so we could brainstorm about how to deal with
common challenges. One principal was facing a no-win
dilemma: "I have a teacher who should be fired, but my hands
are tied. We have documented reports from students and parents testifying to her incompetence. I've arranged counseling,
hired a teacher's assistant, and monitored her classroom. Nothing's helped. She's got two years left to retirement and she's
determined to stick it out and get her full benefits. She thinks
I'm persecuting her and has vowed to file a grievance with the

union and contest this case in court if I try to remove her. What can I do?"

As you can imagine, his conundrum created a heated discussion. The group suggested a variety of approaches, but the beleaguered principal had already tried most of them with no success. In the long run, the group reached a reluctant consensus. A participant summed up the group's feelings. "I've been in a similar situation and I know how frustrating it is. I eventually decided that going through the very lengthy legal process to fire this one teacher was not in the school's best interests. As leaders, we have to make constant judgment calls about what constitutes the best use of our limited resources. My bottom-line decision was, I would rather take the several hundred hours I would have invested in that acrimonious court battle and spend it on the many dedicated teachers who are trying to make a positive difference for their students. My mentor used to tell me, 'No one ever said this was going to be easy. That's why we get paid the big bucks.'" At this, everyone in the room guffawed.

You may be thinking, "That's an awful decision! What if my child was in that teacher's classroom? Are they just going to ignore her incompetence?"

Believe me, the educators disliked this course of inaction as much as you. In an ideal world, the principal would have taken the necessary steps to replace the teacher, her students would have received the quality instruction they deserved, and everything would have turned out copacetic. In the real world, it doesn't always work out that way, as Rabbi Harold Kushner pointed out in his book of this title: *Why Bad Things Happen to Good People.* The principal's reluctant conclusion wasn't a perfect solution to the problem, but it was an informed decision and seemed to be the best alternative of the "pick your poison" options available.

Look Before You Bleep

Some act first, think afterward, and then repent forever.
—CHARLES SIMMONS

This is one of the hardest aspects of dealing with bullies. Sometimes they "win." Sometimes, even when they're clearly in the wrong, we're just not prepared to do what we have to do to deal with them. This isn't fair. In fact, it's quite frustrating. But it happens. And the only way we can live with choosing not to pursue prosecution is to project what would result from challenging this individual. It's better to conclude that it's wiser to walk away up front than regret spending thousands of dollars and months of fruitless effort after the fact.

A friend told me a chilling story of a senior bank officer who didn't look before he bleeped. This executive returned from a week-long professional meeting to discover the bank president had publicly accused him of malingering. Even though his time away had been approved and covered, the CEO had announced that he was off on a boondoggle. The bank officer decided this couldn't go unchallenged. He went into the president's office to complain and was fired on the spot.

This bank manager, who is in his fifties, has now been out of work for months. He has two kids in colleges he can no longer afford; he no longer has company-sponsored health insurance; and he has no prospects in sight. He has almost depleted his savings and has had to put his house up for sale. The last I heard, he was planning to move back to his hometown so he could work in his brother's business.

Act Wisely, Not Rashly

Wisdom consists of the anticipation of consequences.
—NORMAN COUSINS

This is a scary scenario. The rash words of one minute undid a thirty-year career. The thing is, he's not sure he'd do it differently. He certainly isn't glad he got fired, and he isn't glad he and his wife have experienced such bleak months of misery. However, he doesn't regret not playing ostrich. He's not sure he could have lived with himself if he had buried his head in the sand and pretended he didn't know his boss had openly accused him of being dishonest. Perhaps he could have approached his superior in a more diplomatic fashion, but he suspects the outcome would have been the same. The bank president wouldn't have put up with any type of protest, no matter how mild or artfully phrased.

What's the moral of this story? Know the personality of the person you're dealing with and anticipate consequences before inserting foot in mouth.

Do I Want to Ostrich-cize Myself or Risk Ostracizing This Individual?

It seems like one of the hardest lessons to be learned in this life is where your business ends and somebody else's begins.
—KIN HUBBARD, AMERICAN JOURNALIST

Think of a situation in your personal or professional life that isn't right, fair, or kind. If you're being mistreated, you can play ostrich and ignore it, or you can face the situation head-on and hold the individual accountable for his or her actions. The following questions can help you decide whether this is or isn't your business and whether it's in your best interests to make it your business.

Shall I Look Away, Walk Away, or Fire Away?

1. What is this person doing that I find offensive or unfair?
2. Is this person aware that what he or she is doing is unkind, unfair, or inappropriate? Is the behavior intentional or thoughtless?
3. Is this individual's objectionable behavior a one-time incident or ongoing issue?
4. Have I already made reasonable attempts to inform this person of the inappropriateness of his/her actions? Has he or she made any effort to change, or has s/he rejected my verbal olive branch?
5. How is this person's behavior affecting me? Could I be overreacting or is my response justified?
6. Could there be extenuating circumstances explaining his or her behavior that I'm not taking into account? Could these circumstances temporarily excuse how this person is acting?
7. What will happen if I do nothing? Is that an acceptable option? Can I live with myself if I don't speak up?
8. What do I hope to achieve by confronting this person? Be specific. How best can I communicate my message to achieve that goal?
9. What are the risks and potential negative outcomes of confronting this person?
10. Am I willing to pay those consequences? Why or why not?
11. Is there any realistic chance this person will make an effort to improve how he or she treats me and others (voluntarily or involuntarily)?
12. Could pursuing this be a "Don Quixote" exercise in futility? Are the odds that I won't be able to favorably impact this situation no matter how long or hard I try?

13. What are the resources needed to win this "battle"? What will it cost in terms of money, time, emotional toll, legal fees, energy, and brainpower to achieve my desired outcome? This is a measurable question. Figure out in terms of dollars, hours, weeks, months (years?) what it would take to triumph.

14. Is it my job to educate this person? Does someone need to hold him or her accountable, and I'm that someone?

15. Will pursuing this put me at risk or endanger my loved ones? How so? Have I discussed this dilemma with the people who will be affected by my decision? If my efforts don't prove successful, will I and my loved ones regret doing this?

16. Are there other options I haven't explored? Is there a way to address this issue without endangering my job, marriage, family, health, or livelihood?

17. Have I discussed this with a peer or professional who could have innovative, workable insights about how to turn this situation around?

18. Will time heal this wound? Will this situation improve if this individual is left to his or her own "vices"?

19. Are there penalties or advantages for delaying? Do I need to act now? Could waiting help me approach more wisely?

20. Is there an objective third party who could bring impartial perspective to the conflict? Is there a chance someone who's not emotionally involved could mediate a satisfactory resolution? Who is that person and how can I get him/her involved?

Pursue and Persist or Cease and Desist?

Things are never so bad that they can't get worse. But they're
sometimes so bad they can't get better.
—MIGNON MCLAUGHLIN, AMERICAN WRITER

Answering these questions can help you decide whether
engaging in a protracted dog fight is the best use of your time,
energy, talent, and money. A woman named Sandra said, "This
is the thought process our family went through trying to
decide whether to hold our mother's health care providers
accountable for medical malpractice. Our mom had been told
she had multiple sclerosis when she actually had a slow-
growing brain tumor. It was finally correctly diagnosed and the
doctor recommended immediate surgery. Unfortunately, they
were unable to remove the whole tumor, so the doctor ordered
follow-up radiation.

"Our mom did not want to undergo this often debilitating
treatment, but we decided the doctors were the 'experts' and
'knew best,' right? They ended up irradiating the *wrong* spot
and Mom endured weeks of gut-wrenching nausea for nothing. The doctor advised another operation. Once again, Mom
pleaded *not* to be put through this ordeal, but finally suc-
cumbed to the pressure to have the second surgery. It turned
out to be the nightmare she had sought to prevent.

"Over the next few months, there were countless foul-ups.
Staff members were caught smoking marijuana. Mom was left
lying in a hallway for hours following a painful angiogram, and
she almost drowned in her own fluids after an intern misdi-
rected a shunt, draining brain fluid into her lungs. Mom died
the fate she dreaded, hooked up to multiple tubes in the inten-
sive care unit, on a ventilator, and unable to speak.

"Following the funeral, we discussed whether we were
going to file a lawsuit. The doctors may not have been bullies

in the normal sense, but her rights had certainly been violated by this clear case of medical malpractice. In the end, we realized that money wouldn't bring our mother back. We didn't want to profit from her suffering and we didn't want to spend months reliving her pain. We decided the best course of action was to send prayerful apologies to Mom for what she had endured, and to vow that none of us would ever again abdicate our authority or ignore our instincts when making health decisions."

You may be thinking, "What if I ask the 'Shall I Walk Away, Look Away, or Fire Away?' questions and decide I *do* want to tackle this challenge?" The next chapter offers suggestions on how to have the strength of your convictions so you can keep bullies from provoking you.

Action Plan and Discussion Questions

What's an unfair, unkind, or unacceptable situation in your life? What's happening? _____

_____

_____

Review the "Shall I Look Away, Walk Away, or Fire Away?" questions to see if taking action is in your best interests. What are some reasons to follow up on this and what are some reasons to let it go? _____

_____

_____

What did you decide and why? _____

_____

_____

Is there another situation in your life you're not happy with, but you realize it's too big of a risk or not worth your resources to pursue? What is that? Explain your decision.

_____

_____

_____

_____

Summary

HARMFUL BELIEFS/BEHAVIORS	HELPFUL BELIEFS/BEHAVIORS
Pursue without thinking *"I'm going to sue my partner for embezzling that money."*	Think before pursuing *"I'm going to think this through before taking action."*
Waste your resources *"I don't care what it costs; he's not going to get away with this."*	Allocate resources wisely *"I've got to figure out what it will cost in terms of money, time, and the emotional toll."*
Behavior is one-time incident *"I don't care if he intended to pay it back. It was wrong."*	Behavior is ongoing *"His previous partners said he did the same thing to them."*
Don Quixote exercise in frustration *"My lawyers say this could take years because he didn't leave a paper trail."*	Possible to improve situation *"My lawyers say we can check his computer and track his financial withdrawals."*

Confrontation would put us at risk	Conclude that confronting is worth the risk
"He's told me that he'll come after me and my family if I cause trouble."	*"I think that's a bluff and that he's made these empty threats before."*
Act without considering if it's worth our while	Act only if we believe it's worth our while
"I'm going to do whatever it takes to take this guy down."	*"Is this really how I want to spend the next two years of my life?"*

Way 15. Put All Kidding Aside

It disturbs me to learn I have hurt someone unintentionally.
I want all my hurts to be intentional.
—MARGARET ATWOOD, *CAT'S EYE*

AN OFTEN-USED BULLY TACTIC IS TO SAY SOMETHING MEAN AND then follow up with "Just kidding." Bullies claim their dig was unintentional, but it was planned all along. If we protest their thinly disguised insult with "That hurt my feelings," they retort with mock innocence, "Why are you making such a big deal about this? It was only a joke."

Teasing is defined as (1) "to tear in pieces," (2) "to disturb or annoy by persistent irritating," (3) "to attempt to provoke to anger, resentment, or confusion," (4) "to goad," and (5) "to pester." Whew! As you can see there's no *just* or *only* when it comes to teasing.

While it's true that some people's teasing is innocent banter that's part of normal social interplay, bullies use teasing as a passive-aggressive weapon. It's their way of saying something offensive without taking responsibility for the damage they're causing. It's a malicious, indirect way of rousing our wrath and weakening our self-esteem. It's a sneaky way to get our goat while making us a scapegoat for their unresolved anger or envy. What can we do about it? We can take the sting out of poisonous barbs with these "Cease the Tease" steps.

Cease the Tease

If I be waspish, best beware my sting.
—WILLIAM SHAKESPEARE, *THE TAMING OF THE SHREW*

I. **REMOVE THE INCENTIVE.** Teasers do not pick on people who are impervious to their taunts. They target vulnerable individuals who reward them with satisfying overreactions. Stammering, blushing, crying, or becoming offended are all signs of victory to a bully. Desensitize yourself and understand that anything you're embarrassed about is ammunition to a bully. If you're overweight or have acne, you're going to hear about it. A young man I know in Hawaii who's a talented athlete is also pigeon-toed. He says, "It used to bother me when kids gave me a hard time about it, but then I realized I better learn to shrug it off. Now if someone brings it up, I tell 'em they're just jealous because being pigeon-toed lets me grip my board with my toes and gives me better balance surfing."

2. **FIGURE OUT WHAT THE TEASER IS TRYING TO ACCOMPLISH.** Check facial expression to see if the teaser is being playful or punitive. If teasers have a spiteful gleam in their eye, they may be deliberately trying to one-up you. If they have more of a twinkle in their eye, this could simply be an example of their adolescent sense of humor. A teaser is usually trying to rile you by tossing out a taunt that elicits an emotional rebuttal. However, teasing can also be a socially clumsy way of engaging you in conversation and getting your attention. It's an immature "grim and bear it" way to get a reaction,

any reaction, rather than be ignored. This could be an awkward way to try to connect with you.

3. **GIVE THEM A DOSE OF THEIR OWN MEDICINE.** Beating teasers at their own game makes this a losing proposition for them. If you have fun with them, they'll no longer be able to make fun of you. Say, "Hey, it's Teaser Weezer. Or should I say the Teaser Weasel? Okay, give me your best shot. Trot 'em out. Let's see what you've got today." Turn the table on the teaser with "Look who's talking." "Boy, is this the pot calling the kettle black, or what?" If teasers protest, say, "You can dish it out, you just can't take it, is that the way it is?" When you meet teasers tit for tat, rap for rap, they're not controlling the situation, you are.

4. **WORK THE CROWD.** Is the teaser playing to an audience? If there are people around, the teaser is hoping to heighten his or her status by taking you down. The key in this situation is to talk to the group, not to the teaser. "Joe's at it again, picking on people he wishes were his size." In this way you're linking yourselves with them. Now it's not him against you, it's you and the group against him. Outnumbered, he'll probably slink away and think twice before taking you on again.

5. **HEAVE A SIGH AND ROLL YOUR EYES IN MOCK EXASPERATION.** Teasers want to aggravate you. Adopting an "I'm so bored with this" posture frustrates teasers because this is the opposite of what they're trying to achieve. Look heavenward and say resignedly, "Here we go again. This didn't work last time. What makes you think it will work this time?" Meet their attempts to irk you with apathy. A weary "You're wasting your time" will cut 'em off at the pass.

6. **EXPOSE THEIR MOTIVES.** As soon as you take exception to his remarks—"I do not color my hair!" or "I was *not* coming on to you!"—the teaser has succeeded. Instead of going on the defensive, go on the offensive. "Why do you do this? Does it make you feel good to try to make people feel bad? Do you get some kind of cheap thrill out of it?" Uncovering a teaser's agenda and putting her "on trial" will quickly convince her that this is not worth her while.

7. **AGREE AND EXAGGERATE.** One of the best ways to take the fun out of teasing is to immediately agree with a taunt and then add to it. If someone ridicules your lack of computer know-how, say, "Yeah, if someone asks me what kind of computer I have, I say, 'Beige.'" This type of verbal aikido means you don't fight with someone, you flow with them.

One of the best "agree and exaggerate" practitioners I've ever met is former Pittsburgh Steeler quarterback and Super Bowl MVP Terry Bradshaw. Terry is one of the most affable individuals you'd ever want to meet. When people give him a hard time about being "ugly" (he's not), he says, "I'm glad I'm not good-looking. If I looked like Brad Pitt, it'd take me an hour to shave!" If someone gives him grief about his several marriages, his good ole boy response is, "My mama told me, 'You're marrying outside the family—you're gonna have problems.'" If someone ribs him about his supposedly less-than-brilliant IQ, he goes along with it by saying, "Face it, how smart can I be? I made my living by putting my hand on another guy's rear end." Terry makes it difficult for other people to be difficult because he refuses to take himself too seriously.

Is This Person Suffering from Chronic Tease Disease?

*The first thing I do in the morning is brush my teeth and
sharpen my tongue.*
—OSCAR LEVANT, AMERICAN HUMORIST

"My boyfriend is a chronic tease," said a rather soft-spoken
young woman. "He grew up with four brothers, and giving
each other a hard time was just the way they related to each
other. My family, on the other hand, believed children were to
be seen, not heard. The only conversation at our family dinner
table was an occasional, 'Please pass the potatoes.' I've told
Tony I don't like being teased, but he claims it's all in fun and
doesn't understand why I'm so sensitive about it. What can I
do?"

I asked the young woman why she felt her boyfriend teased
her so much. Was it habit, did he feel there was nothing wrong
with it, or was there some hidden agenda? I also asked his
nationality.

She said, "What's nationality got to do with it?" I cautioned
that it's unwise to make sweeping cultural stereotypes because
there are always exceptions, but that it's fair to say that some
ethnic groups are more given to verbal roughhousing than others. "Oh, I see," she said. "Tony's Italian." At that, everyone in
our seminar audience broke into laughter and several said out
loud. "*That* explains it!"

It's common for Italians to have volatile conversations with
much shouting, interrupting, and boisterous opinion-sharing. I
told her, "It's possible that teasing really is second nature for
him and he doesn't mean to hurt you. Maybe you can both
make a compromise. *You* can lighten up a bit and not take it so
seriously and *he* can back off a bit and not do it so much. When
he tosses out a tease, you can come back with a calm 'Could be'
or 'You think?' These 'I'm not going to play' rejoinders could

take the bite out of his verbal grime. Or you could create some return repartee so you give as good as you get. If you feel his comment is a cheap shot, cut him off by saying, '*Cut it out!*' and give him 'the look.' You know the look I'm talking about. The 'I'm not in the mood, don't go there' look."

Are You Gender Tender?

> You know, it's women like you who make men like me
> make women like you make men like me.
> —BOBBY CLARK

Deborah Tannen, the author of the book *You Just Don't Understand*, related an experience she witnessed that added insight into the differences between male-female communication styles. She said, "I was sitting in a plaza on a sunny day watching children play. A little girl was daintily eating her ice cream cone and a boy walked up and pushed her. She immediately started wailing and the girl's mother scolded the 'bad boy' for being so rough. A few minutes later, the youngster spied a boy about his own age on the other side of the plaza. He ran up to the boy and gave him a shove. The boy shoved back. The pair ended up in a tussle and minutes later were happily playing together, having a great time."

Deborah said it was a perfect example of how the impact of behavior can depend more on how the receiver *interprets* it than on how the sender *intends* it. The little girl was hurt by this ruffian's roughhousing; the little boy welcomed it. The little girl's day was ruined; the little boy's day was made.

That's why it's important to ask if our reaction could be a gender issue. What we say is not always what the other person hears. Next time someone says something you regard as offensive, look past the behavior to the intention. Maybe such behavior is this person's socially awkward "stick the little redhead's pigtail in the inkwell" way of getting your attention because he or she wants to connect and doesn't know what to say. Maybe this person's put-downs are a playful cultural or family tradition. Unless this person has a history of being a bully, you might want to give him or her the benefit of the doubt. If, however, you know from previous experience that this person is trying to mess with your mind, use the next idea to be imperturbable.

Talk to the Hand

> Whenever I was upset by something in the papers, Jack always told me to be more tolerant, like a horse flicking away flies in the summer.
> —JACQUELINE KENNEDY

It's a fad these days for kids to make a big display of holding their palm out, looking disdainfully away, and saying with attitude, "Whatever" or "Talk to the hand, because the ears aren't listening." This can be annoying when it is used against us because it's a somewhat rude way of controlling the conversation and having the last word.

There are times, though, when this off-putting gesture is the only thing that will put off a teaser. The outstretched hand may not be polite, but the teaser isn't being polite either. You don't want to thrust your hand in a teaser's face because that is an offensive challenge. Simply raising your hand about shoulder-high will usually cause him or her to stop mid-sentence, which is what you want. The other person will probably pause for just a moment, and that's your chance to get your verbal foot in the door.

Don't Bite the Bait

A fishing rod is a stick with a hook at one end and
a fool at the other.
—Samuel Johnson

Another way to make a teaser stop in his tracks is to make a T
with your hands in the time-honored way of calling "time-
out." Then, like a referee, say "Stop right there!" and call him
on his verbal infraction. Say "Knock it off" or "You agreed
you weren't going to do this."

Be sure to use the teaser's name. Why? People prick their
ears up when you preface your comment with their name
because it lets them know this remark is intended directly for
them. Picture someone in your life who may be a little rough
with you verbally. Imagine yourself holding your hand up and
saying, "Rob, cut it out! I'm not in the mood" or "Mandy,
don't even try this with me."

Bullies tease to test your pluck. Pluck is defined as "fortitude
or strength of mind that enables a person to encounter adversity with courage." Instead of taking their remarks personally,
understand that they don't necessarily believe you are stupid,
ugly, or whatever—they're just calling you names to make you
crack under their pressure. Let teasers know they're out of luck
if they try to test your pluck. Simply say "Nonsense" or "Hog-
wash" and then move the topic on to something else.

Take the advice of a country gentleman who had his own
method for dealing with teasers. He said, "When someone tries
to give me a hard time, I think of the wise old bass who lives in
a pond on my property. He knows a baited hook when he sees
one, and so do I. My mamma didn't raise no fools. If someone's
fishing for a reaction, no way am I going to open my big
mouth and swallow their hook. They can dangle all the bait
they want. I'm not biting."

Action Plan and Discussion Questions

Do you have someone in your life who likes to tease you? What kinds of things does he or she say? _____

_____

_____

Do these remarks bother you? Why or why not? _____

_____

_____

What is his or her intent? What does he or she hope to accomplish? _____

_____

_____

From now on, what is one specific way you're going to "cease the tease"? Are you going to give them the look or use a hand gesture (no, not that one!) to stop them in their verbal tracks? Explain. _____

_____

_____

Do you agree it helps to have some rejoinders at the ready so you don't bite a teaser's bait? What are you going to say (for example, "That's ridiculous and you know it") next time someone tries to hook you with a barbed remark? _____

_____

_____

Summary

HARMFUL BELIEFS/BEHAVIORS	HELPFUL BELIEFS/BEHAVIORS
Teasing is no big deal *"She says she's joking, so I guess I shouldn't take it seriously."*	Teasing can be hurtful *"I don't care if she says it's a joke. It's mean."*
Overreact and bite the bait *"Hey, I have not had my nose fixed."*	Desensitize self *"If I'd had my nose fixed, would I have chosen this one?"*
Make fun of you *"What a perky nose."*	Have fun with them *"That's Miss Perky to you."*
Teaser playing to audience *"What's next—you going to lose those love handles?"*	Turn audience against teaser *"Cara's at it again, folks—putting other people down so she can feel better about herself."*
Get riled up *"I hate it when you do this."*	Become bored with it all *"Grow up."*
Address the content *"This is my real nose, honest."*	Address the intent *"Are you thinking of some plastic surgery yourself?"*
Test our pluck *"Why don't you leave me alone?"*	Talk to the hand *"Whatever."*

Way 16. Act On (vs. Act Out) Your Anger

I was angry with my friend: I told my wrath, my wrath did end.
I was angry with my foe: I told it not, my wrath did grow.
—WILLIAM BLAKE

"I'M NOT ANGRY," I INSISTED. "I JUST DON'T WANT TO HAVE ANY-thing to do with this person." The therapist nodded knowingly and jotted some notes on his pad.

Therapists know that people who insist they're not angry . . . are. They may have stuffed their anger so deep they don't know it exists. They may even complain of depression, not knowing that depression is often an indication of sup-pressed rage.

It's time to understand that anger is a natural response to our rights being trampled. It's actually the way our emotional sys-tem is supposed to work. If someone does something hurtful to us or to someone/something we love, our mind gets mad as a way of signaling "That was wrong." Anger is the original warning system for letting us know our line's been crossed.

Unfortunately, many of us have been intellectualized out of our anger. Anger isn't pretty. It can lead to yelling and scream-ing, which isn't "nice," so we mentally ratchet it in rather than run the risk of letting it out and saying something we regret. My *Tongue Fu!* book featured many quotes about anger, almost all of them involving negative connotations. For example:

- The greatest remedy for anger is delay. —Seneca
- If you are patient in one moment of anger, you will escape a hundred days of sorrow. —Chinese proverb
- For every moment of anger, you sacrifice sixty seconds of happiness. —Dale Carnegie
- Anger is never without a reason, but seldom with a good one. —Benjamin Franklin

These quotes are insightful, but there are times when it's right to get angry. There are times we'll actually produce more sorrow if we don't speak up. An angry response can be more effective than a reasonable response when dealing with bullies.

Temper, Temper

> If you're not outraged, you're not paying attention.
> —MAL HANCOCK

The problem is, many of us have internalized these cautionary quotes to such a degree that we perceive all anger as bad. We bury it, deny it, and think we've failed if we can't rise above it. After years of doing our best not to feel this dark emotion, we stop feeling it. We become numb inside because we have dulled this turbulent emotion that scares us to death.

It's time to understand what a terrible price we pay for believing we don't have the right to be angry. Believing this is tantamount to believing we don't have the right to feel aggrieved. It means that if people hurt us, we're somehow supposed to take the high road and continue to respond rationally—no matter what. In other words, be a saint.

Many of us believe deep down that anger is a base emotion that only "un-evolved" people show. Enlightened folks are supposed to be peaceful and loving, right? An enlightened, loving spirit is indeed a worthwhile goal. An equally worthwhile goal is recognizing we have the right to *not* be loving when someone is being lethal to our physical and mental health. It's time to stop apologizing for honest anger and start expressing it responsibly so we no longer suffer in silence when we are wronged.

I'm not suggesting we go around losing our temper at the slightest provocation. I'm suggesting that justifiable outrage is sometimes justified. Shakespeare said, "To be furious is to be frightened out of fear." Our goal is to no longer be fearful of becoming (when the situation warrants) furious.

I'm Mad as Hell, and I'm Not Going to Take It Anymore

> The silent bear no witness against themselves.
> —ALDOUS HUXLEY

The silent also bear no witness *for* themselves. As explained before, quiet endurance of bad behavior condones it. The "mad as hell" line above is from a climactic scene from the movie *Network* when a frustrated broadcaster sticks his head out the window and screams his frustration to the world. His pent-up outburst may have made him feel better, but it didn't help his cause, because it was reactive anger. Reactive anger means letting loose pent-up fury without considering the consequences. Responsible anger is thinking first and articulating what's on our mind and in our heart in an effort to improve our circumstances. Acting out anger means unleashing mindless rage at someone who did something we *didn't* want. Acting on anger means articulating feelings in a mindful way and asking for what we *do* want.

Express A.N.G.E.R. Constructively

It is easy to fly into a passion. Anybody can do that. But to be angry with the right person and to the right extent and at the right time and with the right object and in the right way—that is not easy, and it is not everyone who can do it.
—ARISTOTLE

These five steps can help us express A.N.G.E.R. constructively rather than destructively so we can be angry with the right person to the right extent in the right way.

A = ASSESS WHAT HAPPENED. Ask yourself, "Why exactly am I upset?" Pinpoint the cause so you know what's making you mad. Did this individual break a promise? Did he or she say something derogatory about you or a loved one? Is this person not giving you enough attention? Are you angry at yourself because you made a mistake and you're embarrassed? Identify the reason behind your anger so you can target the wrong that needs to be righted.

N = NO EXTREME WORDS. Extreme words produce extreme reactions. *Always, nothing, never, no one,* and *everyone* are sweeping generalizations that incite emotion. If we say, "You *never* listen to me," the other person will huffily point out the one exception that disproves our claim. "Please wait until I'm finished talking" will get better results than saying "You *always* interrupt me." Saying "We agreed to stick to our budget this month" is more constructive than "You always overdraw our account."

G = GIVE SPECIFIC EXAMPLES. The more precise you are, the more productive you'll be. If you describe exactly what was done or not done, the other person knows what not to repeat.

Sweeping accusations such as "You are *so* irresponsible" are open to interpretation and don't isolate the particular act/inaction that caused the problem. Say instead, "When I got home tonight, dishes with food had been left on the living room floor and ants were crawling all over them."

E = EXPRESS THE BEHAVIOR *WANTED* IN THE FUTURE. Once you give evidence of what was wrong, *move on*. Complaining about what has already happened won't undo it. Instead of punishing people for past mistakes, pinpoint how they can perform better in the future. Say, "I want to be able to trust you. From now on, please rinse your dishes and put them in the dishwasher as soon as you finish eating. It's the only way we can prevent an ant problem." As my dad used to say, "We can't motivate people to do better by making them feel bad." Focus on desired outcomes (what we *do* want) rather than dreaded outcomes (what we *don't* want).

R = REVIEW TO MAKE SURE YOU GOT THROUGH. Trying to have the last word or warning, "This better not happen again" leaves a sour taste and little incentive for the other person to cooperate. Asking "What's your understanding of this?" or "How are you going to do this differently from now on?" gives the other person a chance to verbally commit to changed behavior.

Anger Is One Letter Short of Danger

> People can't walk over you unless you lie down.
> —ANN LANDERS

The heading above is yet another example of the bad rap anger gets. From now on, understand that not acknowledging and articulating honest anger is what's dangerous.

"I was one of those people who was afraid to get angry,"

Tricia said. "I don't explode, I implode. My parents fought like cats and dogs. I would lie in bed with my pillow over my ears and mentally beg them to stop. I vowed never to be like them. I went a little overboard, though, and was so nice to everybody all the time that I got walked on a lot. I finally snapped last year when one of our PTA officers went too far one too many times.

"I was president of our local elementary school PTA. Our program chair was notoriously lax about her responsibilities. I don't know why she volunteered for the position because half the time she didn't show up for the meetings. What's worse is that half the time the speaker she scheduled *also* didn't show up for our meetings. Patti called me two hours (two hours!) before our December program, traditionally our biggest event of the year, to say the parenting expert she had booked wasn't going to be able to come after all. Before, when things like this happened, I would just take charge and let her off the hook. Not this time. I was absolutely clear this was her responsibility.

I told her, 'I am really angry that you waited until the last minute to tell me about this. Patti, you need to find a substitute, quick.' She whimpered, 'But how am I supposed to find someone? It's four o'clock and the meeting starts at six.' I said, 'Figure it out, and you better find someone good because we've got three hundred people showing up at the school cafeteria in an hour and a half, and if you haven't found someone, you're going to be the one to explain it to them.' Then I hung up. That felt so good. Patti must have done some scrambling because a former school counselor gave a wonderful program on how we could (guess what?) hold our kids responsible. Needless to say, Patti never tried to pull that again."

Kudos. Next time you feel that unsettling emotion in your gut that signals you've been wronged, don't disregard it. Use the A.N.G.E.R. steps to constructively express what you're feeling so the situation is addressed instead of ignored.

Action Plan and Discussion Questions

When was the last time you got angry at someone? How did you handle it? Did you yell and scream? Suffer in silence? Keep your cool and assert your rights? Explain. _____

_____

_____

Did you grow up thinking anger was a normal part of relationships or something to be afraid of? Elaborate. _____

_____

_____

Is there a situation in your life right now that's making you mad, but you've been afraid to admit it? What is that? What steps are you going to take to correct it? _____

_____

_____

In the future, how do you intend to act on (vs. act out) your anger so you deal with this emotion in healthy ways? _____

_____

_____

Summary

HARMFUL BELIEFS/BEHAVIORS	HELPFUL BELIEFS/BEHAVIORS
Anger is to be avoided *"Getting upset won't help."*	Anger is to be acknowledged *"I have a right to be angry."*
Reactive emotions *"I'm going to let her have it."*	Responsible emotions *"She needs to know that was wrong."*
Act without thinking *"I'm so mad at you I could spit."*	Assess before acting *"How can I talk about this in a way that it never happens again?"*
Extreme words *"What was on your mind? You never think, do you?"*	Accurate words *"Annie, taking the car without permission was wrong."*
Give sweeping generalizations *"I'll never be able to trust you again."*	Give specific examples *"Barbara said she saw you driving down Main Street this afternoon."*
Express what you don't want *"You do this one more time and you're grounded for life."*	Express what you do want *"From now on, if you want to use the car, you need to ask the night before."*
Wrap up with a threat *"I've asked the neighbors to keep an eye on you, so don't think you can try this again."*	Review to make sure you got through *"What's our agreement, and what's your understanding of the consequences if you don't honor it?"*

Way 17. Bid Adieu to Dr. Jekyll and Mr./Ms. Hyde

Let me introduce myselves.
—SCOTT FRIEDMAN, HUMORIST

SHORTLY AFTER MOVING TO THE EAST COAST, I READ A FASCINAT-ing article in *The Washington Post*. A columnist told a story on herself about how we often don't follow our own advice. As a financial counselor, Michele has repeatedly instructed readers to never give private information over the phone. On this particular day, she had gone to the gym for her daily workout. She walked out of the health club only to find her car window shattered and her purse gone. Devastated, she still had the presence of mind to report the theft to her bank and credit card companies.

A short while later, she received a call from her bank manager on her cell phone (which she'd kept with her). He explained they had caught the burglar trying to use her ATM card. Relieved, Michele burst into tears. She was especially appreciative of the manager's solicitous manner. He asked for a few details so he could confirm her account information, explaining he wanted to make sure the thief didn't have an accomplice who would try to use her card at another branch. Thankful for his thoroughness, she gave him the information and promised to meet him at her bank as soon as she could get there.

As she started driving, it struck her. She had given a stranger her PIN number. Dumb, dumb, dumb. She arrived at her bank and (you saw this coming, didn't you?) confirmed her worst fears. No one knew what she was talking about. The person she had talked to was the thief, not the bank manager. And yes, in the short time it had taken her to realize she'd been had, he had withdrawn the maximum amount of funds from her account.

The columnist couldn't believe she had fallen prey to such an old trick. She was especially angry with herself because she realized the reason she never suspected the truth was the caller had such a courteous, urbane voice. She realized that somewhere in her mind, she must have thought that someone with such a sophisticated, caring manner could never be a crook.

Welcome to the world of Dr. Jekyll and Mr. Hyde. As the movie of that title so impressively shows, good and evil can exist in the same person. This can be a hard thing to wrap our mind around because we tend to think of people as good or evil, not both. Remember the old nursery rhyme "When she was good, she was very, very good; and when she was bad, she was horrid"? Well, that's how Jekyll and Hyde personalities work. They are one person in public and another in private.

Bullies Are Masters of Deception

> There's only two things I don't like about him. His face.
> —DOROTHY PARKER

Don't you just love serendipity? I took a break from working on this chapter to take a walk/talk around our neighborhood lake. I picked up my mail on the way in and found that week's issue of *People* magazine waiting for me with an article about this very topic.

The article, entitled "Painfully Privileged," interviews author Susan Weitzman about her book *Not to People Like Us*. Her book addresses a surprising bias that she discovered through her counseling practice. Namely, that society doesn't believe domestic abuse happens to middle and upper class women. Her research has revealed just the opposite—that up to 60 percent of the women in her practice have suffered from what she calls upscale violence. She says many of these women are successful in their own right, hold at least a bachelor's degree, and live in a household with a combined income of $100,000 or more.

The article makes the point that not only does society discount this as a possibility; the victims themselves don't believe it's happening because they've never been exposed to abuse before. They are bewildered that someone who supposedly loves them can at the same time be so cruel. Weitzman explains that many of these women are accomplished high achievers who have never had anyone be mean to them. They conclude they must be doing something wrong and redouble their efforts to "fix the problem." Further complicating the issue is the fact that these women are confused. On one hand, their spouses are charismatic, contributing community citizens in good standing, many are even active in their church. On the other hand, these same "role model citizens" are capable of shocking brutality.

One of the terrifying aspects of these on-off personalities is you never know which one you'll wake up to, which one you'll come home to, or which one will walk in the door. This means you live on a constant roller coaster of apprehension. Anyone who lives or works with this type of individual never knows what's coming next. Things can be going swimmingly, and the next thing you know you're in hot water.

Who Are You Today?

The bad times I can handle. It's the good times that drive me crazy.
When is the other shoe going to drop?
—ERMA BOMBECK

A psychologist friend once reported an interesting finding she'd heard at a conference she'd just attended. The lecturer had said that children are remarkably resilient and can learn to cope with almost any parenting style (short of out-and-out abuse) . . . as long as it's consistent. What's actually more difficult to deal with is a parent who's affectionate one day and heartless the next.

Children never feel secure with this type of "hot-cold" behavior because they don't know if what they were allowed to do yesterday will be punished today. Anxiety can be defined in two words: not knowing. Not knowing if their next word or action is going to change their just-moments-ago loving mother or father into a raving lunatic keeps these children in a never-ending state of emotional limbo.

Sound familiar? Those who live or work with a Jekyll and Hyde often end up being nervous wrecks. Since they can't predict what will set their volatile partner off, they don't know how to prevent it from happening. They monitor everything they say lest they trigger a tirade. They often end up "dulling themselves down" to minimize the chance they'll do something the bully will find offensive and use as an excuse to turn on them.

Outsiders Look Askance at the Accuser, Not the Abuser

> In France, they ignore those who set fires and
> punish those who give the alarm.
> —NICOLAS CHAMFORT, FRENCH WRITER

As you can imagine, this guessing-game lifestyle takes a toll. To make matters worse, people on the outside often tell J & H victims how "lucky" they are. Acquaintances only see the public behavior of Mr./Ms. Hyde, which is purposely kept "perfect," so everyone wrongly concludes they're a "perfect" couple.

Partners of J & H bullies rarely go public because their accounts of abuse are met with skepticism. A horrifying reality is that if victims finally dare to speak up about their torment, people tend to discredit their "outlandish" charges against this "pillar of the community." Whistle-blowers are often the ones pilloried instead of the one doing the damage. The sad fact is that people who are not privy to what goes on behind closed doors tend to look askance at the accuser rather than the abuser. At some level, people simply can't or don't want to believe that an acquaintance they admire could be capable of atrocious behavior.

What's worse is that police can take action only if there's tangible evidence of a crime. This makes trying to hold a Jekyll/Hyde accountable even more of a no-win proposition, because verbal abuse does not leave physical marks. It leaves emotional scars (sometimes for decades after the fact); but since psychological wounds cannot be visually substantiated, somehow they don't count. The deliberate destroying of a human being's spirit can't be proven so it goes unpunished. Furthermore, the bully has often warned the victim not to report him or her or else. The victim is frightened into silence because s/he knows from experience the abuser has the obsessive determination to make good on his or her threats.

No More Martyrs

There is a time for departure even when there's
no certain place to go.
—TENNESSEE WILLIAMS

So what to do? Decide that your mental and physical health is a higher priority than the "false" security of a marriage, house, and income—especially if that marriage, house, and income come attached with an abuser. Realize that your sanity and safety are more important than maintaining the status quo. It's especially important to realize that if you have children, staying in this relationship means you're teaching them this is what marriage is like and this is how men and women treat each other. You're teaching them that a parent's role is to martyr him or herself and to silently suffer and stay in a relationship—no matter how horrible.

Is that what you want your life to be? Is this what you want as your future? Is this what you want your children to mimic—because they will. If you've been telling yourself that maybe he or she will change, they won't. Research shows again and again that abuse doesn't "go away" of its own accord; it escalates. As a psychologist explained, "It is better to be from a broken home than in one."

Fact is More Fascinating Than Fiction

The truth is the one thing nobody will believe.
—GEORGE BERNARD SHAW

Ready for a "fact is more fascinating than fiction" story? Several years ago while still living in Maui, I decided on impulse to get a haircut. I stopped by my favorite place (a hair salon overlooking the ocean—such a deal) and, as luck would have it, my stylist had an opening. This stylist/salon owner has a great chairside manner and I soon found myself telling him about some of my recent woes. He said, "I don't know if you believe in this stuff, but my roommate is a psychic and I'd love for you to meet her."

Guess who walked in the shop two minutes later? Yup, his roommate. She said, "I was driving by and thought I'd drop in to see if you wanted to have lunch." My stylist looked at me in amazement and said, "She's never done this before." His roomie looked at me and said, "Why don't you join us?" and then she looked at the receptionist and said, "And why don't you come, too?" The receptionist protested, "I can't leave. We'd have to close up the shop." To which my stylist said, "Why don't we do that? We'll close the shop, and all go to lunch." (Ah, the joys of being an entrepreneur, and remember, this was Maui!)

The salon owner locked up and we walked over to the beachside restaurant, all of fifty yards away, and sat at a big circular table. We shared preliminary chitchat for a few moments and then my stylist told his roommate a little of what I had been going through. She looked me straight in the eye and said, "That's not all that is happening, is it?" I confessed it wasn't and shared some of the more private details of what had taken place in the last few months.

This perceptive (or prescient) woman shook her head in accepting amazement and said, "I guess I'm supposed to tell you my story," and proceeded to do just that. "I was one of the millions of married people who thought divorce was not an option and that it was important to 'keep the family together at all costs.'" She added, "And I know how trite that sounds."

"Statistics backed me up," she said. "Our father always played devil's advocate around the dinner table and taught us to defend our decisions with logic, so I placed an inordinate amount of importance on what the 'experts' said. Study after alarming study showed that there was no such thing as an ami-cable divorce for children and that they suffered devastating consequences years after the fact because us parents couldn't get our act together and behave like grown-ups. I was deter-mined to do everything I could to provide a healthy home for my kids so they would have a good upbringing."

Statistics Do Lie

When I can no longer bear to think of the victims of broken homes, I begin to think of the victims of intact ones.
—Peter deVries

The roommate continued. "Over the years, my husband became increasingly abusive toward me, but I told myself I was an adult and I would put up with it as long as the kids weren't being harmed. Then I discovered that my husband, the same man who had all these pictures of himself with politicians and celebrities on our walls, was not really in construction, as I had believed all our married life. He was connected to the mob." (Sounds like the Sopranos, doesn't it?)

This woman realized her kids *were* being harmed by this imposter. "I told him I had found him out, and that I was leav-ing and taking the kids with me. Big mistake. He warned me that if I even thought about leaving, he would have me declared insane and put away—and I knew he could do it."

Is It Time to Throw the Bully Out with the Bathwater?

> Looking back over the years we've spent together, I can't help but
> wonder, "What the heck was I thinking?"
> —INTERNET GREETING CARD

This terrified woman left in the middle of the night with her five (!) children, drove cross-country, and lived, frugally and incognito, on the West Coast until her kids were grown. She said, "My children constantly thank me for having the courage to do what I did. My three sons are all married and they are wonderful to their wives. My two daughters don't let anyone mistreat them. I guess that's my legacy. My advice to anyone who is in an abusive relationship is 'You may not know how you're going to pull it off and it may be very hard, but you will never regret leaving. You will only regret not leaving . . . sooner.'"

Meeting that woman was a gift and her advice was right on. Are you living or working with a Dr. Jekyll and Mr./Ms. Hyde? Is it time to throw the bully out with the bathwater? Or if you can't get the bully out of your life, are you going to get out of his or hers?

Way 28, "Screw Up Your Courage," shares some tips on how to get yourself out of an abusive relationship. For now, simply ask yourself if staying or leaving is in the best interests of you and your loved ones.

Action Plan and Discussion Questions

Do you work or live with a Dr. Jekyll and Mr./Ms. Hyde personality? Who is that person? _____

_____

_____

What's an example of their public behavior and what's an example of their private behavior? _____

_____

_____

Have you decided that the bad outweighs the good? Do you believe this person would ever change or that circumstances could improve? Why or why not? _____

_____

_____

Has this person made threats against you? Are you afraid he or she will retaliate? Are you afraid that people won't believe your version of events? Elaborate. _____

_____

_____

Are you ready to get out of this relationship—even if there are risks? Do you believe things will get worse, not better, and that it's in the best interests of you and your loved ones' safety and sanity to leave? Explain. _____

_____

_____

Summary

HARMFUL BELIEFS/BEHAVIORS	HELPFUL BELIEFS/BEHAVIORS
Charming in public, cruel in private *"Good-bye, thanks for the nice party." "You stupid cow."*	It is not acceptable for anyone to abuse you—ever *"I am not going to allow him to berate me like this."*
Live in anxiety because can't predict how he or she will act from moment to moment *"Go to your room and keep your voices down. Your dad has been drinking again."*	You have the right to be with someone who is consistent and reasonable *"Why should we have to hide in our own home? I'm going to talk to him about AA tomorrow."*
Afraid to speak up *"If I say anything they're going to think I'm crazy."*	Need to speak up *"I need to tell someone so I'm not alone with this nightmare."*
Confused because s/he is both cruel and kind *"Yes, s/he hits us sometimes, but s/he doesn't really mean it."*	Occasional kind behavior does not cancel out cruelty *"Hitting is never acceptable under any circumstances."*

Way 18. Don't Leave Home Without It

Serenity comes not alone by removing the outward causes of fear,
but by the discovery of inward reservoirs to draw upon.
—Rufus Jones

A FRIEND DIAGNOSED WITH ADHD, ATTENTION DEFICIT
HYPERActivity Disorder, says he has the attention span of a
gnat. For years, he searched in vain for something that would
help him counteract his nervous energy. After trying Ritalin,
hypnosis, biofeedback, and just about everything else, he
finally discovered something that helped control his fidget-
ing . . . a rosary.

He carries it in his pocket wherever he goes. If he's in conversation and his thoughts are flitting here and there, he works
his worry beads to quiet his mind and give his hands something to do. "Sitting through a movie or a long meeting used
to be the impossible dream," he said. "I don't mean to be sac-
rilegious, but using this rosary gives me an outlet for my impa-
tience so I can stay focused for more than five minutes without
totally losing it."

You may be wondering, "That's nice, but what has this got
to do with bullying?" If it worked for him, it can work for us.

We too can design and draw upon our own "reservoir of serenity" to keep us calm and make us strong.

Take Your Touchstone

> Look well into thyself; there is a source of strength which will always spring up if thou wilt always look there.
> —MARCUS AURELIUS

While browsing for a gift in a Saratoga Springs boutique, I spied a lovely tigereye in the shape of a heart. I knew instantly it was what I wanted to give this friend because it's a tangible embodiment of what it means to be a samurai.

This young person was trying to find his way in the world. He was a gentle soul, and gentle souls sometimes don't do too well in the teenage world. In high school, where rowdiness rules, he was often "odd teen out." Sometimes I could see his confusion when he watched the in kids with their loud, brash ways. Their constant competing to rearrange the popularity pecking order simply wasn't him. He wanted to be included, but didn't want to abandon who he was and become like these wild and crazy guys. There didn't seem to be any middle ground.

That's where the heart rock came in. It's a visual reminder that we can be nice *and* strong. This valentine-shaped stone was loving proof that we can be both solid as a rock and a soft touch. These contrasting qualities can coexist in the same person, as they do in this "soft rock."

This weekend, check out a museum shop, nature store, or a craft boutique. Find a beautiful stone that is lovely to behold. Carry it with you in your purse or pocket so you have a tangible talisman to keep you strong in stressful situations. When dealing with challenging individuals, wrap your hand around it to remind yourself you can be hard if necessary without losing your heart. If you're around someone who used to push you around, use it as a visual reminder to be rock-solid. You can even be immovable if that's what the situation calls for. Knowing your heart's in the right place can give you courage to stand firm.

Are You Shell-Shocked?

> Reality leaves a lot to the imagination.
> —JOHN LENNON

One of the by-products of being in a battle with a bully is that it's easy to start living in our head. Like a tongue probing a sore tooth, we can't stop thinking about the latest insult or outrageous affront. The problem with this is, the more we replay the tapes of what they've said and done, the more shell-shocked we become. Their destructive influence begins to infiltrate our every waking moment. This, of course, is exactly what bullies want. Their goal is to dominate our thoughts.

Our goal is to stay grounded in reality so bullies can't take over our life. One way to do this is to surround ourselves with tangible reminders of the still-wonderful world that exists outside the tyrant.

Friends on Maui had a nightmarish experience with a private contractor who'd been hired to remodel their home. After several delays, the builder had basically demolished one section of their house and then absconded with the money they had foolishly prepaid him for supplies. Not only were they out the $20,000 they had planned for the project, they had several unusable rooms with structural damage where interior walls had been torn down.

My friends couldn't get past this debacle because every time they walked around their house, they were reminded what a mess they were in.

My friend told me about this during a walk/talk on one of Maui's user-friendly beaches. After hearing her tale of frustration, I suggested we start keeping our eyes on the sand. She asked why and I explained that I used to get homesick when I was on the mainland on a long speaking tour. One morning while on my beach walk, I had discovered a small white curved seashell that fit perfectly on the end of my thumb.

I asked Janice, "You've heard of a thumbnail sketch? Well, this became a thumbnail shell. From then on, I kept one of these shells in each pocket of my outfits. If I was missing my sons or was troubled about something, I would slip it on my thumb and instantly be back home imagining myself walking by the ocean while Tom and Andrew boogie-boarded, happy and carefree." I suggested that Janice could do the same. If she started getting upset about the damage done by the contractor, she could slip her thumbnail shell on for perspective and focus her attention on all that's right with her world instead of what's wrong.

Have a Tangible Talisman

> I don't care about that, it rolls off my back like a duck.
> —SAMUEL GOLDWYN

Talisman is defined as "an object held to act as a charm to avert evil and bring good fortune." What tangible talisman could you use to keep your mind on your fortunes (perhaps your health, loved ones, freedom to change your circumstances) rather than your fear? What object can you hold to avert those evil images and memories so they roll off your back like a duck?

One woman going through a nasty divorce kept a picture of her two children in her Day-Timer, on her desk, and on her car dashboard. Whenever she was despondent and wondering if she had the will to put up the good fight against her powerful ex-husband, she would look at their faces and remind herself of her determination to be strong for herself and for them.

Another carried a piece of paper with the words "Stay strong. You can't help anyone else unless you save yourself" in her pocket. Whenever she felt herself wavering she'd hold the paper in her hand and silently repeat the message on it until her resolve revived. "In my weakest moments," she said, "when I would question whether I had the courage to do this, I would just touch the note and be comforted. It was more of a touch-paper than a touchstone," she said with a smile, "but all the same, it was a lifesaver."

Carry the Strength of Your Convictions

> The willingness to accept responsibility for one's own life is the source from which self-respect springs.
> —JOAN DIDION

Inspirational quotes can also help us face adversity with courage. In the middle of a crisis, we can take a minute to read the words of someone who has triumphed over tragedy to remind us that we can do the same. That person's example can keep us from sliding back down the slippery mental slope of despair. Select one of the following messages (or find one that resonates with you) and make several copies. Post the message where it will be in sight, in mind and tape it with you by affixing it to an index card that you keep in your wallet. Next time you're between a rock and a hard person, pull out your good pluck charm and give yourself the strength of your convictions.

- "The very least you can do in your life is to figure out what you hope for. And the most you can do is live inside that hope. Not admire it from a distance, but live right in it, under its roof." —Barbara Kingsolver

- "There are always two voices sounding in our ears—the voice of fear and the voice of confidence. One is the clamor of the senses, the other is the whispering of the higher self." —C. B. Newcomb
- "Courage consists not in hazarding without fear, but being resolutely minded in a just cause." —Plutarch
- "You've got to own your days, each one of them, every one of them, or else the years go right by and none of them belong to you." —Herb Gardner
- "An individual dies . . . when, instead of taking risks, he cowers within, and takes refuge there." —E. M. Cioran
- "I need to take an emotional breath, step back, and remind myself who's actually in charge of my life." —Judith M. Knowlton

Give Yourself an Instant Attitude Adjustment

He's just one man.
—LINE FROM THE PLAY *JESUS CHRIST SUPERSTAR*

When we're dealing with an ogre, it's easy to forget he or she is just one person. It's hard not to be consumed by the not-so-mellow drama. Allowing that to happen would be a shame, because it means the bully has accomplished what he/she set out to do—ruining our life.

Let's not give them that power. Let's turn our thoughts to the people we love instead of the person we'd love to hate. Staying in touch with our heart rock and heartfelt message can remind us, even in the midst of misery, that somewhere the sun is still shining, children are still playing, and flowers are still blooming. Our touchstone can give us instant perspective and shrink this problem or person down to their deserved minuscule size. In that way, we take back control of our life and goodness prevails.

Action Plan and Discussion Questions

Do you already have something that serves as your talisman or touchstone? What is it, and how does it help you maintain peace of mind? _____

_____

_____

If not, when and where are you going to acquire a "soft rock" to give yourself tangible evidence that you can be loving and strong at the same time? _____

_____

_____

Do you find yourself obsessing about how a difficult individual has treated you? Explain. _____

_____

_____

How are you going to keep in touch with reality? Is there a quote or message you could post and carry with you to focus your thoughts on what's right with your world instead of what's wrong? Explain. _____

_____

_____

Summary

HARMFUL BELIEFS/BEHAVIORS	HELPFUL BELIEFS/BEHAVIORS
Worrywart *"I always feel so intimidated at these holiday office parties."*	Worry beads *"I'm going to take my rosary so I can soothe my stress."*
Hate to be hard *"Bob is getting too close again and backing me up against the wall."*	Can be hard without losing heart *"Bob, I think I see your wife over there trying to get your attention."*
Don't know where we'll find our strength *"He's my husband's boss— I don't want him to get mad at Mack."*	Gain strength from our good pluck charm *"I know I can handle him without making a scene."*
Out of touch and losing conviction fast *"Oh, no. He's been drinking. This is getting out of control."*	Take our touchstone to have courage of our convictions *"Bob, keep your hands to yourself or you'll have to explain this to the CEO."*
Obsessing about what's wrong *"This is so revolting. Why did he do this to me?"*	Quotes help us focus on what's right *"There are no victims without volunteers. I can handle this."*

Way 19. Refuse to Play the Blame-Shame Game

When my mother makes out her income tax return
every year, under Occupation she writes in,
"Eroding my daughter's self-esteem."
—ROBIN ROBERTS

BULLIES ARE MASTERS AT HOLDING OTHER PEOPLE RESPONSIBLE FOR their misbehavior. Instead of claiming "The Devil made me do it," they argue, "*You* made me do it."

Blamers purposely go on the attack so you end up defending yourself instead of asserting yourself. They know that by focusing the fault on you, they keep it off themselves. They would rather erode your self-esteem than admit they made an error. If you're planning to confront a blamer about his or her actions, it's important to know this in advance so when he or she tries to turn the tables on you, you're prepared for it.

How to Hold Your Own When Holding Blamers Accountable

> To err is human. To blame it on someone else is politics.
> —HUBERT HUMPHREY

To err is human. To blame it on someone else is predictable. Here's how you can hold blamers accountable for mistakes.

1. **USE AS FEW WORDS AS POSSIBLE.** The wordier you are, the weaker you come across. Succinctness connotes confidence.

2. **DON'T LISTEN TO REASON(S).** Bullies always have rationalizations for why they did what they did. Think what the word rationalize means: "rational lies." It's not that they were late. No, traffic held them up. It wasn't that they were rude. No, it was that "uppity salesclerk" who made them lose their temper. It wasn't that they didn't deserve the promotion. No, it was that lousy supervisor who played favorites. Bullies always have a reason for everything, and none of them have anything to do with them.

3. **APPEAL TO A BULLY'S NEED TO SAVE FACE, NOT TO ANY SENSE OF FAIRNESS.** Trying to point out to a bully that what he or she is doing is morally wrong can be a waste of time. The only thing that motivates bullies to change their behavior is seeing that they will suffer in some way if they don't stop. Bullies respond to negative consequences. Only when we reverse the risk-benefit ratio and they realize they're about to be penalized for their inappropriate actions will they choose to act differently.

    A friend of mine who runs a large nonprofit agency told me of the time their newly appointed board president set up his own interview with the local newspaper and made numerous commitments on behalf of their organization. "The other board members were aghast that he had spoken out of turn and didn't clear his comments ahead of time. Their initial attempts to convince him he was getting ahead of his team were dismissed.

"It was clear this loose cannon wanted to make his mark by wielding the influence and taking advantage of the attention that came with his position. It was only after our previous president pointed out that this guy was going to end up censured by his own organization that he toned down his lone wolf act. Pleas for politically correct leadership had gone ignored. The only thing that convinced this ambitious individual to be more circumspect was pointing out that he was about to be publicly embarrassed for making unfounded claims."

4. **GIVE THEM AN OUT.** Since appearances are so important to bullies, it's smart to give them a way they can justify in their own minds that this was their decision to take responsibility and do things differently. Remember the young lady samurai at the beginning of the book who told her father, "I'm proud of graduating from Georgetown. If you're here to help me celebrate, you're welcome to stay. If you're not, leave." By giving bullies two options, both of which are acceptable to you, instead of an ultimatum and letting them choose which course of action they're going to take, they can comfort themselves with the perception that they're still in charge.

5. **ACT OUTSIDE OF THEIR EXPECTATIONS.** Sometimes we've got to be wild and crazy to get a bully's attention. They may be so accustomed to ruling the roost, they don't even listen to anything we say anymore. A social worker who was supervising a shift at a juvenile detention home said two teenaged girls really got into it. They were wrestling on the

floor, pulling each other's hair, and punching each other. Nancy said she tried to pull them apart, to no avail. Several other employees joined the fray in an effort to stop the cat-fight, with no success. Finally, at the end of her rope, Nancy started *screaming* at the top of her lungs. The two teens stopped trying to hurt each other and stared at her in amazement. Nancy said, "I don't even know why I did it, but it worked."

Plan to Be Unpredictable

> Truth is might and will prevail. There is nothing
> the matter with this, except that it ain't so.
> —MARK TWAIN

Why did this work so well? Nancy had done the unexpected. When dealing with bullies, we need to act outside our customary range of behavior or we'll get the customary results. We can tell the truth until we're blue in the face and it won't get through a habitual blamer's mental armor. Surprising them with unanticipated behavior forces them to come up with a new response. We're not doing same old, same old, so they can't either.

Since blamers count on us being reasonable, we may need to be unreasonable. Since blamers count on us to be rational, we may need to be irrational. Since blamers count on *us* to shoulder the responsibility, we need to make *them* shoulder the responsibility.

Remember earlier in the book when we discussed how our strength taken to an extreme can be our weakness? Many of us are empathetic to a fault. Oops, look at that language. We are empathetic *to a fault*.

Don't Let Yourself Be Used as a Human Garbage Disposal

> I have had enough.
> —GOLDA MEIR

A woman named Lisa said, "My roommate complained constantly about her job. She would itemize every little thing that had gone wrong, rehashing incidents and obsessing about what each person had said or done. A recurring theme was that everyone was a foul-up except her.

"When she had finished bashing everybody, she'd waltz off and I'd be left sitting there, down in the dumps. If I ever dared to suggest that she might be playing some role in all this and her censure was a little one-sided, she'd turn on me with 'Oh, great! So now my own roommate is criticizing me? Who else am I supposed to talk to if I can't talk to you?'

"I wish I'd known about the Rights/Needs Seesaw because it would have helped me see how one-sided her behavior was. Five minutes into it, I would have told her 'Enough!' and gotten up and walked away. She probably would have called me a few other choice names, but that would have been better than sitting there and letting her turn me into her own private dumping ground."

Can You Say Unequivocal?

> I know she's outspoken, but by whom?
> —DOROTHY PARKER

One of the best ways to persuade blamers to put a sock in it is to stand up and say "Enough!" The one word "Enough" is perfect because it's brief and it's unequivocal.

Unequivocal is such a great word. It means definite, explicit, incontestable, unambiguous. These are all the things we want to be when dealing with outspoken people who find fault with everyone but themselves. Remember, bullies and blamers are full of intensity, and in a confrontation between intensity and uncertainty, intensity almost always wins. That's why we need to speak with self-assurance. When they sense that we're unequivocal instead of ambiguous, they're not so quick to dump on us because they know we have a mind of our own. (What a concept!)

From now on, understand you do not have to patiently listen to faultfinders who are bending your ear (and will). One way bullies control us is by taking up our time. Think about it: the blamer plays the dominant role, the listener the passive role. Bullies control the situation (and you) by commanding your attention—whether you want to give it to them or not.

Off-loading problems on others is not appropriate—unless it's complicit. To expect people to stop everything and listen to them orate ad infinitum is insensitive at best, selfish at worst. Only a bully would do this repeatedly, and only a bully would accuse you of being a lousy listener if you're unwilling to be a mute audience to his or her monologue.

As comedienne Paula Poundstone said, "I think we need a Twelve Step group for nonstop talkers. We're going to call it On and On Anon." The next time someone starts talking on and on and on, cut 'em off. This may come across as politically incorrect, but continuing to give them a sympathetic ear will perpetuate their whines and reasons. As Gertrude Stein said, "Let me listen to me, not to them." And if a trash-talker in your life doesn't like it, remember the word "Tough."

Control the Conversation

---

*Tact is the art of putting your foot down without
stepping on anyone's toes.*
—LAURENCE J. PETER

If someone has consistently been over-the-top tactless, it's appropriate to put your verbal foot down even if it does step on toes. There are times when it's appropriate to control the situation, because if we don't, the other person will.

A security manager said, "You're right about not letting blamers get a word in edgewise. I handle a lot of the discipline problems for our organization. Believe me, these people always have a hundred and one reasons why whatever went wrong wasn't their fault. When I sit down with repeat offenders, I don't even let them get started on the whys and wherefores. If I start listening to their excuses, we'll be there all day."

He continued: "If I don't control the conversation, they will. They do this by counterattacking. I had a woman in here who insisted it was unfair to blame her for pilfering hundreds of dollars of office supplies because 'everyone else did it' and there wasn't a rule forbidding it in the employee handbook. She was trying to make me out to be the bad guy in the situation."

He's right. Blamers purposely put us in a position where we are so busy denying their criticisms, we forget what we claim for. Their goal is to make us feel guilty so they don't have to.

Detach, Don't Debate

Not only did he not suffer fools gladly; he did not suffer them at all.
—LESTER B. PEARSON

One of the most important ways to cancel the blame–shame game is to detach instead of defend. As discussed earlier, manipulators know that if they blame you for an error, you'll be tempted to deny it. As soon as you do, they have succeeded in changing the subject and moving the spotlight off them and onto you.

The following are a variety of phrases you can use to deflect blame and shame. Remember, bullies can't play us like a foot if we don't argue with their untrue accusations.

BLAME AND SHAME	DETACH, DON'T DEBATE
"You blew it. You should have started this weeks ago."	"You're entitled to your opinion."
"You're such a slob. You should take better care of yourself."	"You're not going to draw me into this."
"You never think of anyone but yourself. You're so self-centered."	"It's too bad you see it that way."
"You never gave me a chance. You had already selected someone for this job."	"That's your opinion."

Don't Open Mouth, Don't Insert Foot

> It's a common delusion that you can make things
> better by talking about them.
> —DAME ROSE MACAULY HARRY

Remember, if a bully attacks with "You love your ex-boyfriend more than you do me," don't protest with "That's not true!" If you do, he has just succeeded in engaging you in a "Yes, you do; no, I don't" debate. Instead say, "We agreed that discussing previous partners serves no one. That topic is off-limits." If the bully persists with "You're laughing in all your pictures with him and you never laugh when you're with me," say, "Drop it. We're not going there." Notice these responses are short and they don't challenge the content of what the other person is saying. Notice that you don't wait until the other person stops talking (that could be a *long* time). If you're dealing with someone who, as John Mason says, "talks at the drop of a pause," you need to interrupt and cut 'em off before they build up a head of blame-shame steam. They can't sell you a ticket for a guilt trip if you don't buy it.

Action Plan and Discussion Questions

Can you think of a time you bought into a bully's blame-shame game? What happened? _____
_____
_____

Is there someone in your life right now who is a habitual faultfinder? How are you going to detach instead of debate his/her unfounded accusations? _____
_____
_____

Do you deal with someone who blames everyone for his/her problems? Do you continue to listen empathetically? What are you going to do next time he or she starts talking on and on and on? _____
_____
_____

Do you sometimes buy tickets for guilt trips? How so? What will you do next time someone tries to make you feel bad for not giving in to his or her demand? _____
_____
_____

Summary

HARMFUL BELIEFS/BEHAVIORS	HELPFUL BELIEFS/BEHAVIORS
They hold *you* responsible *"It's your fault our checking account is overdrawn."*	You hold *them* accountable *"Janice, take responsibility for your own actions."*
They have 101 reasons why everyone else is to blame *"This wouldn't have happened if you knew how to balance a checkbook."*	Don't listen to whines or reasons *"Wait just a minute here. Don't say something you'll regret."*
Appeal to their sense of fair play *"It's not nice of you to say this is my fault."*	Appeal to their need to save face *"Review the checks before you start laying blame."*
Act in predictable ways *"I can't believe I'm crying and that I let her get to me."*	Act unpredictably *"Look me in the eyes and apologize RIGHT NOW!"*
Count on our empathetic listening *"She hasn't let me say a word."*	Cut into the monologue *"Enough! It's my turn!"*
Debate *"I'm tired of doing this every month."*	Detach *"You're not going to draw me into this."*

Way 20. Ask, "Is What I'm Preaching What I'm Teaching?"

The only rational way of educating is to be an example—
if one can't help it, a warning example.
—ALBERT EINSTEIN

FOR MONTHS I'VE ASKED JUST ABOUT EVERYONE I ENCOUNTER, "Can you think of someone who bullied you? What did he/she do? How did you respond? What worked? What didn't? Were you finally able to resolve the situation? How?"

A friend who writes a nationally syndicated column for teachers reported this unsettling story. This educator was asked by a couple what they could do about their daughter, who was terrified of an extremely aggressive classmate who had targeted her. The parents said the twelve-year-old (!) bully-ette's behavior went beyond adolescent name-calling and teasing. Her systematic scheming was downright diabolical.

The parents had already complained to their daughter's homeroom teacher. The teacher confronted the taunter, who not only denied any wrongdoing but had the audacity to accuse their daughter of making it all up in an effort to cause trouble because she was "so unpopular." The parents took their case to the principal, who essentially shrugged it off with "Your daughter needs to learn how to handle this kind of stuff because it happens all the time. We can't watch them every minute."

The parents were at their wit's end. They said, "Our daughter comes home every day crying and begs us not to make her go back. She has stomachaches every day and is losing weight." At this point, my educator friend interrupted and said simply, "Take her out."

You'll never guess what the parents' response was. "We can't take her out. This school has the best reputation in the area and we've already paid tuition for the whole year." After further discussion, my friend sadly concluded that this couple seemed more concerned about their pocketbook and their daughter's continuing to attend this prestigious school than they were with her psychological well-being.

This former school principal suggests that parents look at themselves and ask, "What are my actions or *non*-actions teaching my children?" The disconcerting message being sent to this poor girl was "Status and money are more important than standing up for yourself."

She added, "It's true that kids need to learn how to deal with teasing. It's also true that parents need to act on their children's behalf if they're suffering from outrageous abuse at the hands of someone else. Can you imagine how this twelve-year-old must have felt? She must have felt that no one was listening to her, that no one really cared, and that she was all alone with no options."

Way 26, "Give Schoolyard Bullies an Education," will provide specific suggestions on how children can protect themselves from playground bullies. For now, if you're a parent the question is, whether or not what you're preaching is what you're teaching? If you're a manager, what message are you sending your employees? If you're in a relationship, what signals are you sending your partner?

What We Accept, We Teach

In influencing others, example is not the
main thing; it's the only thing.
—ALBERT SCHWEITZER

A friend told me about an encounter she had as a child that
negatively influenced her for years. She was ten years old and
lounging in her favorite summer hangout, the town's air-
conditioned library. She had walked there from her home, a
few blocks away. She was looking something up in the card
catalog (yes, this was a long time ago) when a man walked over
and stood next to her. She looked up, puzzled, wondering what
he wanted. He pushed a piece of paper into her hand and
motioned her to look at it.

As soon as she saw what it was, it was as if he had hit her. He
had drawn a crude picture of her in the nude, with an obscen-
ity coming out of her mouth. She was so shocked, at first she
didn't know what to do. Then she ran out of the library and all
the way home. Sobbing, she stumbled into the house, found her
mother, showed her the picture, and told what had happened.
Who knows whether her mother had had a bad day or just
didn't know what to say? Whatever the reason, she folded the
picture up, put it in a drawer, and told her daughter to stop crying. That was the end of that. Except it wasn't. My friend said
the silent message her mother sent was "When somebody does
something bad to you, put it away in a drawer, stop crying, and
don't say anything about it."

My friend told me, "It's taken me years to undo that lesson.
I wish my mother had done something. I wish she had taken
me into her arms. I wish she had called the library to report
what had happened so the staff would watch for that man and
keep him from traumatizing any other unsuspecting children. I
wish she had sat me down and said if anything like that ever

happened again, I should immediately go to the nearest adult and tell him or her what had happened. I wish she had done *something*—even if she didn't know if it was the right thing. Because the message I internalized was that this was my fault. I felt dirty, like I'd done something wrong to deserve this."

That mother was probably just overwhelmed at the moment and didn't understand that her lack of action would have long-term consequences. The point is to understand that if we do nothing when someone mistreats us or a loved one, we teach the perpetrator that it's acceptable, and we teach ourselves and the people around us that passively enduring mistreatment is the proper response.

Is that the message we want to send to bullies, ourselves, and loved ones? I think the message we want to send is "*No!* You cannot do this and get away with it. I will *not* look the other way. I will speak up. You will be held accountable." In the long run, this is the only way to convince bullies it's not worth-while.

Fools Rush In

Any fool can condemn, criticize, and complain, and most do.
—DALE CARNEGIE

"I agree with this," said one woman. "My daughter plays travel team softball in California. We go to tournaments almost every weekend, and last year the team made nationals. Even though these girls are only fifteen or sixteen years old, many of them are already being scouted by colleges.

"Last year, the girls' coach really had a mouth on him. He had played in the minors and took the game very seriously. He was constantly screaming at the players, even at his own daughter, who was the star pitcher. When team members would go up to bat, you could see how nervous they were by how they hunched their shoulders and kept glancing over at him. Players who made errors dreaded going back to the dugout because they knew they were going to get bawled out.

"His rampages made several of us bleacher-warmers uncomfortable, but none of us dared say anything because we were afraid he would retaliate against our daughter and not play her.

"One weekend the father of one of our players came to a game for the first time and sat next to me in the stands. I could tell he was steaming after the coach ridiculed his daughter for flubbing a throw. He waited until the game was over and then went up to the coach and asked to speak to him in private. I heard this through the grapevine, but I guess he told the coach in no uncertain terms that an adult man calling a teenaged girl an idiot and telling her 'Your stupid mistake just cost us the game' was verbal abuse even if it was happening in an athletic arena."

Verbal Abuse Is Wrong—No Exceptions

> Few are willing to brave the disapproval of their fellows,
> the censure of their colleagues, the wrath of their society.
> Moral courage is a rarer commodity than bravery in battle
> or great intelligence. Yet it is the one essential vital quality
> for those who seek to change the world.
> —ROBERT KENNEDY

Kudos to this father for having the moral courage to speak up instead of S.I.S. (Steaming In Silence) as he witnessed the coach's atrocious behavior. He was absolutely right to call foul, and absolutely right in his assessment that verbal abuse is unacceptable regardless of where it's taking place.

I hope coaches everywhere understand how wrong it is to vent rage on their players. Doing so teaches young people that it is "normal" for adults to howl at them and that they (and their parents) are supposed to endure this abuse and not say a word in defense of themselves. Is this what we want to teach our sons and daughters? Do we want them passing this message on to future generations? Because they will. What is done *to* our youngsters will be done *by* our youngsters.

Show a Little R-E-S-P-E-C-T

Boys will be boys, and so will a lot of middle-aged men.
—KIN HUBBARD, AMERICAN JOURNALIST

You may be thinking, "Every coach, male or female, yells at his or her players. That's what coaches do." It may be true that this is the norm. Does that mean it's a good thing? Does it make sense to condone ridicule just because it's common? When are we going to understand that verbal abuse is every bit as damaging as physical abuse? When are we going to take a stand and no longer look the other way when adults direct their rage at defenseless children?

If you've watched youth sports, you know it's not just the coaches who get carried away. You've probably witnessed over-ambitious parents who persecute their kids for blowing a big play. You've probably seen overzealous fans get wrapped up in the game, and the next thing you know, they're screaming at five-year-olds, "Lazy! Stupid! What a dumb mistake!" I remember an article in the *Los Angeles Times* that reported more than 60 percent of kids give up organized sports by the time they're twelve years old. Why? The number one reason given was that they were tired of adults yelling at them. Isn't that a sorry state of affairs?

Cheer, Don't Jeer

If you're not miserable, you're not practicing.
—CYNTHIA LEVIN

It's time to practice common courtesy instead of making young athletes miserable. We can stem the tide of temper tantrums if we personally commit to lobbying for change in our local school sports programs and hometown recreation leagues. Some communities have already taken the lead. They've instituted "quiet games" where parents vow not to say a single word from the stands or sidelines. The kids love it! Perhaps you can follow the example of that brave father who collared the softball coach. Perhaps you can speak up at your next league or team meeting and ask everyone to shape players instead of shame them by contributing cheers, not jeers.

Can you imagine the powerful message we would send by caring enough to hold ourselves and other adult authority figures accountable for treating children with the respect they deserve? We would be saying, "How we treat each other matters. Communication counts. We will speak to each other with R-E-S-P-E-C-T."

Action Plan and Discussion Questions

Do you know someone who is mistreating the people around him or her? Are you bearing silent witness? If you're not speaking up or taking action, what message are you sending? _____
_____
_____

Does your lack of action sanction this bully's behavior? Is it time to intervene, as this father did, so the people involved know their verbal abuse will not be tolerated? Why or why not? _____

_____

Does this unacceptable situation demand some moral courage for you to speak up? How can you summon up the strength to do so? _____

_____

Whom are you going to contact (coach, athletic director, school principal) to propose that treating young people with respect be mandated behavior? How are you going to lobby for this issue so children will be treated with R-E-S-P-E-C-T? _____

_____

Summary

HARMFUL BELIEFS/BEHAVIORS	HELPFUL BELIEFS/BEHAVIORS
Ignore the issue when something bad happens *"It's none of my business if that coach shoved his player against the fence."*	Address the issue when something bad happens *"Coach, keep your hands off that young man."*

Do nothing when bullied *"It's not my place to speak up."*	Do something when bullied *"I'm going to stop this."*
Steam in silence when we witness verbal abuse *"I can't believe he's giving that kid such a hard time."*	Speak up when we witness verbal abuse *"Coach, you need to cool off and calm down."*
Believe that screaming at kids is an adult's right *"I don't like it, but I guess my coaches yelled at me, too."*	Send the message that it's our right to be treated with R-E-S-P-E-C-T *"I'm going to call the recreation director tonight and ask for a parents meeting."*

Way 21. Ask Yourself, "Is This Deja Moo?"

I told my doctor I broke my leg in two places.
He told me to quit going to those places.
—HENNY YOUNGMAN

YOUNGMAN'S QUIP IS FUNNY; IT ALSO HAS POTENTIAL FOR ADDED insight. Modify it slightly and ask yourself, "Do I keep going back to people who break my heart?" If so, quit going back to those people!

Friend and fellow speaker Scott Friedman has a different way of expressing this. If a perennial bully is giving us a hard time, he suggests we ask ourselves, "Is this deja moo? Have I heard this bull before?" If this person has a history of abusing us, why are we climbing back into the bull ring with him or her again? Or, as my friend expresses this, "Insanity is continuing to do the same thing and expecting a different result."

What's Your Return Policy?

*Family reunions are that time when you come face-to-face with
your family tree and realize some branches need to be cut.*
—RENÉE HICKS

A young woman shared this story: "My mother-in-law is
manic-depressive. When she is in her 'down' phase, she is rather
introverted. When she's in her manic phase, especially if she's
not taking her meds (she hates them because they make her
'numb'), she turns into Attila the Hen.

"I'm a Realtor, so I'm gone a lot on weeknights and weekends showing houses. I'm good at what I do professionally, but
I don't have that same level of confidence about parenting. Half
the time I don't know if I'm doing a good job, and the other
half of the time I feel bad for not being there for my kids as
much as I'd like. She knows I'm sensitive about this and seems
to purposely target my anxiety about it.

"My husband, Carl, has told me over and over that I can't let
her get to me. The saving grace for him is that after one particularly vicious episode in which his mother told him she regret-
ted the day he was born, his saint of a father took his son's face
in his hands and said, 'Look me in the eyes and remember what
I'm telling you. Your mother's behavior is *not* your fault, and
there's nothing you can do to make her better.'

"My father-in-law had nailed it. Carl had always believed
that if he just tried hard enough, researched long enough, or
experimented with enough different approaches, he'd finally
be able to reach his mom and she would turn into June
Cleaver. His dad finally convinced him that his mom was not
going to change and he had to stop giving her the power to
devastate him. Carl still cares for his mom, but he's developed a
thick skin and no longer lets her criticism get through.

"She's in her manic phase right now and is 'hell on heels.'

She gets obsessed with projects, and yesterday her project was me. She sent this blistering e-mail that carried on about how our kids were spoiled little brats who were going to grow up to be monsters, and how I should stick to real estate and leave the parenting to someone else. It shattered me.

"My husband came home and found me weeping. I told him what had happened. He listened for a while and then said something that stopped me in my tracks. He asked simply, 'Why did you read the e-mail? You know what she's like.'

"I looked at him, dumbfounded. He wasn't being mean, he was just gently prodding me to realize that I had in a way played a role in this. Why had I read the e-mail? I knew she was in a manic phase. I knew these missives of hers were often vicious. Why had I reopened myself to her mean-spiritedness? My husband was right. I was culpable."

Hope Springs Eternal

Hope begins in the dark, the stubborn hope that if you just try to do the right thing, the dawn will come.
—ANNE LAMOTT

Why do we do this to ourselves? Why do we let people back in who have hurt us before? Many of us want to believe that they will come to their senses, feel remorse, and opt to be kinder. Some of us still care and want to give them one more chance to change their evil ways. And some of us simply can't comprehend that human beings can consciously choose to be cruel even when it's to everyone's detriment, including their own.

There's a well-known parable about this. An alligator was preparing to cross a river when a scorpion appeared and asked for a ride. The alligator snorted, "You've got to be kidding. I'm not going to give you a ride. You'll sting me." The scorpion protested, "Why would I do that? I want to get across the river as much as you do." "No way," the alligator resisted. "I can't trust you." The scorpion reassured him, "Look, if I sting you, we'll both drown. Now why would I do a stupid thing like that?" The alligator grudgingly admitted the truth of this and agreed: "Okay, get on." The scorpion got on and the alligator crawled into the river. Halfway across, the scorpion stung the alligator. Shocked and dying, the alligator asked disbelievingly, "Why did you sting me? Now we're both going to die." His passenger, going down for the last time, gargled out, "I'm a scorpion. That's what I do."

Scorpions Sting Eternal

> Why, since we are always complaining of our ills, are we constantly
> employed in redoubling them?
> —VOLTAIRE

You've heard the adage that "a tiger doesn't change his stripes"? Well, scorpions don't change their stings. The way to stop scorpions from zinging us is to stop giving them rides on our back!

If someone in your life is sending you hostile e-mails or leaving you obnoxious voice mail messages, remind yourself that you are not obligated to read or listen to them. If someone has hurt you time and time again, stop inviting this person back into your head.

Follow the advice of a woman who finally took action to stop her ex-husband's persecution. "My former husband and I share custody of our children. They spend two weeks at his house and two weeks at mine. What complicates matters is that we both travel, so we often need to make changes in our schedule. On top of that, he's always late with his child support and alimony checks and I've got to keep after him to make those payments. That requires a lot of messages being sent back and forth, and he used to fill them with these venomous attacks. He'd bury some important detail in the middle of the call or at the end of an e-mail so I'd be forced to read or listen to the whole thing to find out what I needed to know.

"My divorce attorney recommended I copy his e-mails and record his phone messages so the court would have documentation of his harassment. My lawyer then drafted a letter informing my husband that from that day forward, his written and spoken communication to me needed to address only the logistical information concerning our children or financial arrangements. At the first derogatory word or opinion, the phone call would be terminated or the e-mail would be printed for our files and then deleted but not read.

"He tested this, of course, and claimed it was my fault our kids didn't get registered for summer camp because I had failed to sign and submit the application form he had attached to one of his hateful e-mails. My attorney copied him with his original message showing it had been deleted after the first name-calling paragraph. Every once in a while, he'll try zapping me again. However, the second he starts in, I cut the communication off."

Click Off the Remote Control

> Never give up and never give in.
> —HUBERT HUMPHREY

Sometimes we give scorpions the ability to sting us even when they're not in the same room. I remember reading a fascinating article about a world-famous model who had spent a good deal of her adult life under the thrall of a Lothario who controlled her (almost) every move. In this interview, she related how she was on a shoot in Europe and was still letting this individual rule her life even though she was thousands of miles away. Out on the town one night with the crew, a photographer asked her something and she responded, without thinking, that so-and-so wouldn't let her do it. The photographer asked in wonderment, "What kind of power does he have over you?!"

Indeed. Do you have someone in your life who tries to control your every waking moment? Do you find yourself saying things like "She wouldn't let me do this"? "He made me turn that job offer down"? "She told me I couldn't go"?

Are you an adult? Why are you letting someone tell you what you can or can't do? Why are you allowing someone to make you do things you'd rather not do? Why are you permitting someone to pull your strings as if you were a puppet? Don't you have a mind of your own?

If you are in a relationship, by all means, coordinate your actions with those of your partner. However, don't let other people make your decisions for you and don't let other people run your life. The question is, "What do *you* think?" "What do *you* want?" "What do *you* believe?"

Be the Final Authority on Your Own Life

> My wife and I have a perfect understanding. I don't try
> to run her life . . . and I don't try to run mine.
> —ROBERT ORBEN

Instead of giving away your power and living a life not your own, have clarity that you are a grown-up and are going to act like one. That means you treat people as equals, not superiors. It means you have the final say-so concerning what you do and don't do in your personal and professional life. It's time to act like a samurai and take back the remote control. Resolve to push your own buttons and pull your own strings.

One woman sighed upon hearing this idea and said it had given her much-needed perspective on her relationship. "I never realized how insidious his control of me has become. The words *let* and *make* have indeed crept into my vocabulary. He makes me drive his old pickup truck to work when I hate it because he says he needs the family car. He makes me accompany him on weekends and sit around while he flies model airplanes all day with his friends. He doesn't let me take night classes even though I really want to.

"I'm a middle-aged woman. Why do I let him force me into all these things? Because I'm afraid of him. He's never hit me—well, physically he's never hit me—but [her eyes open in amazement as she realizes this] he hits me with words all the time. I shrink in his presence. It just seems easier to go along with him because he gets so ugly if I don't."

Who's at the Wheel of Your Life?

When you look in his eyes, you get the feeling
someone else is at the wheel.
—DAVID LETTERMAN

Not only will the meek not inherit the earth, they won't inherit much of anything. Next time a bully tries to tell you what to think or do, pull a deja boo. S/he doesn't have a ghost of a chance of controlling you if you stop putting her or him on a pedestal. Say to yourself, "This person is my *equal*, not my superior. My opinions count just as much as his or hers, not less or more."

This woman doesn't have to put her husband down; she's just no longer going to let him put her down. She could say, "If you want to own a pickup, then you drive it from now on." "You're welcome to go with your friends to the model airplane field this weekend, and I have other plans." "I'll be taking night classes, so I'll be gone on Tuesday and Thursday evenings."

The Little Princess Circle

Never pay any attention to the critics—don't even ignore them.
—SAMUEL GOLDWYN

Do yourself a favor this weekend and rent *The Little Princess* video. It's a poignant portrayal of someone summoning up the courage to confront a bully who has been terrorizing her. Through a series of circumstances, this young girl is taken to a school run by a cruel headmistress. The jealous woman locks the bewildered young girl in the dark, spooky attic, but not before deliberately frightening her by announcing that her life as she knew it was over. The young girl curls up on the hardwood floor and weeps. Through her tears, she notices a piece of chalk and a light flickers in her eyes. She picks the chalk up, laboriously draws a circle around herself, and then settles back down on the floor inside her protective cocoon.

This is all done in silence, but it's evident that the girl is establishing a boundary to block out the woman's hateful energy. Later in the movie, the resourceful little princess stands up to the headmistress and realizes, in what is called in Hawaii a "chicken skin" moment, that the schoolmarm no longer has any power to hurt her. The movie makes a powerful statement about how we can maintain our sense of self when dealing with someone who's determined to break our spirit.

If you're dealing with someone who's trying to destroy your spirit, could you draw an imaginary safety circle around yourself and picture their sarcastic or sadistic remarks deflecting harmlessly off your protective cocoon? Could you hold this image in your mind and imagine their criticism being unable to penetrate your plastic bubble? Take back responsibility for your life and refuse to let someone make you mad, sad, or depressed. You don't have to disparage them, just don't let them disparage you.

Action Plan and Discussion Questions

Do you have someone who has been sending hateful communication to you? Have you continued to take the calls or read the messages? Why? _____
_____
_____

Is this person a scorpion? Do you anticipate he or she will continue to sting because that's what scorpions do? Explain.
_____
_____

How are you going to turn "deja moo" into "deja boo" and stop this person from poisoning you? _____
_____
_____

Do you find yourself saying "he/she won't let me do this" or "he/she made me do this"? Who is this person and why have you given him or her the remote control of your life? _____
_____
_____

How have you been culpable in this situation? How are you going to start acting like a samurai on your own behalf? ___
_____
_____

Summary

HARMFUL BELIEFS/BEHAVIORS	HELPFUL BELIEFS/BEHAVIORS
Oh no, more deja moo *"My brother is in jail and wants bail money again."*	No more deja moo *"My brother needs to learn a lesson. No more bail money."*
It's all his or her fault *"When is he going to grow up and take responsibility?"*	I could also be at fault *"I wish I had talked with him earlier about getting help."*
Stung by a scorpion, again *"I can't believe it. I got him out of jail and he's taken off."*	Don't give scorpions a ride *"Yes, I know this means you're going to stay in jail."*
Bully has remote control *"I can't stop wondering where he is and worrying what he's up to."*	Take back your own control *"He's forty-five years old and needs to look after himself."*

Way 22. Depend on the *Kinkiness* of Strangers

I have always depended on the kindness of strangers.
—Blanche Dubois in Tennessee William's
A Streetcar Named Desire

A FRIEND WAS DRIVING HOME THE BACK WAY WITH HER TEN-
year-old daughter when she saw a man viciously slapping a
woman and throwing her against a wall. The man was screaming obscenities at her and the woman was trying to ward off his
blows.

Without a second thought, Victoria stopped the car (this was
on a dark street with no one else around), ordered her daughter
to lock the doors, and ran over and yelled as loud as she could,
"What are you doing? Stop this right now!" The man stopped
and turned to her, startled. Much to Victoria's shock, the
woman, with tears and blood streaming down her face, said,
"He's my boyfriend. Leave us alone."

Victoria walked back to the car, dumbfounded. She started
driving home, but had to stop a few blocks later and pull over
to the curb because she was shaking (and shaken) so badly. She
was mortified, not just because of the unexpected reaction of
the woman with all its ramifications, but because she realized

she had put herself and her daughter at risk by intervening.

The moral of this story? You have nothing to gain and a lot to lose by confronting someone who's violent. What if you're not given a chance to get away? What if you're cornered by someone who intends to physically bully you? The following tips can help you handle dangerous situations so you can, hopefully, get out of them intact.

Rally Your Resources

Fear is a kind of bell or gong which rings the mind into quick life on the approach of danger. It is the soul's signal for rallying.
—HENRY WARD BEECHER

A woman named Laura said, "A co-worker in my building was raped in the parking lot after she left work late one night. Our company sponsored a self-defense class for all women employees in an effort to prevent that type of thing from happening again. They brought in a police officer, a karate instructor, and a consultant who specializes in executive protection. Those classes were such an eye-opener for me. One of the most important things I learned is that you can't take for granted that you'll stay safe as long as you stay out of 'dangerous' areas.

"I had always thought, in a kind of unarticulated way, that as long as I didn't wander around some parking garage at midnight or walk down deserted streets, nothing bad would happen to me. Wrong. The policeman told us many assaults happen in innocent circumstances, like when you're taking your groceries out to your car in broad daylight." The following tips can help us act quickly on our own behalf if put in danger.

Stranger Things Have Happened

If the creator had a purpose in equipping us with a neck,
he surely meant us to stick it out.
—ARTHUR KOESTLER

1. **STAY ALERT.** Would-be assailants look for people who appear distracted because a preoccupied person can be easily over-powered. You're a prime target when you are sitting in your car talking on your cell phone, searching through your purse, or entering something into your Palm Pilot because you're unaware of your surroundings. Pay attention when you're in public places so you won't be caught off guard.

2. **CARRY AND DISPLAY A DETERRENT.** Contrary to popular thought, keys are not a deterrent because you have to get up close to use them. Leave at least one hand free so you can defend yourself if necessary. If you're carrying packages in both arms, it's hard to fight back. It's better to make several trips than to be burdened down with several full shopping bags. Carrying an umbrella or a can of pepper spray gives you something to fend off an assault. Blowing a whistle or sounding the emergency alarm button on your keys can at least alert anyone in the vicinity that something's wrong.

3. **GO WITH THE CROWD.** There really *is* safety in numbers. If leaving a theater or shopping center, walk to the parking lot or garage with other people. If you're by yourself, do not open your car doors from a distance with your remote because it signals which vehicle is yours and lowlifes can slip in the back door and hide. Don't be embarrassed to ask security personnel to walk you to your car if you're in an isolated area. Don't take the stairs in empty buildings. Yes, it's

nice to get exercise, but some stairwells are notorious hang-outs for predators.

4. **FIGURE OUT WHAT THEY'RE AFTER.** Most criminals want either to snatch your purse or wallet or to hijack you to a secluded location where they can take their time with you and don't have to worry about getting caught. If you think they're after your money or property, drop both on the ground, say "Take it," and run in the other direction. You can always replace your credit cards, checkbook, etc. If they're after *you*, get tough. This is not the time to be sweet. The more difficult you are, the more discouraged they'll become. If you cause a commotion, assailants looking for an easy target will probably decide this is too time-consuming and you're not worth the trouble.

5. **GET MAD AND BAD.** Do not say something timid like "Please don't hurt me." Those meek words incite criminals because they show you're scared. If someone starts coming toward you, hold your hands out in front of you and yell, *"Stop!"* or "Stay back!" or "I have pepper spray!" Instead of pleading, "Leave me alone," go on the attack with words like "Go away!" If they try to grab you, yell "Fire!" or "Fight!" because people pay more attention to that than they do to "Help!" Some security personnel believe bystanders run away when they hear "Fire!" but run toward you when they hear "Fight!" because they want to watch. Whatever you do, don't scream helplessly. Roar in RAGE.

6. **DON'T PLAY BY THE RULES AND DON'T TRY TO REASON WITH THEM.** If you are grabbed, do not play fair. Go for the groin or stick your fingers in his eyes *hard*. If he grasps your hands, twist your wrist toward you because that can break his hold. Bend his fingers back. Stomp his feet with your heels. Bite exposed body parts. Scratch his face with your nails.

Kick vulnerable areas like the knees. Toss propriety out the window and become a raving maniac. Trying to talk some sense into him—"You don't want to do this"—won't get through. He is in a predator-like state and not in his right mind. It won't help to beg for mercy or appeal to logic or humanity. At the moment, he doesn't have any.

7. **RUN FOR YOUR LIFE.** Whatever you do, don't let them drag you into a car or van. You'll be in even more danger if they succeed in taking you out of sight and away from witnesses who could intervene or at least report what's happening. Some security specialists suggest that even if the person has a gun, it is better to take your chances and *run.* They say that policemen miss their mark a large percentage of the time when shooting at a moving target from more than twenty feet away. They feel your odds of surviving are actually better trying to escape than going with someone who has a weapon.

8. **GO WITH YOUR GUT.** If you're about to get on an elevator by yourself and a suspicious-looking stranger steps on, step out and wait for another elevator. If someone knocks on your door, says his or her car is broken down, and asks to come into your house to use your phone, and it feels wrong, it probably *is* wrong. If someone appears to be following you, move out of the shadows and walk out in the open where you can't be yanked into an alley. Some police officers suggest you boldly whistle or sing out loud—anything to break the silence, which may be interpreted as fear by a criminal. If your insides are churning, there's usually a legitimate reason. A fellow professional speaker who is a security specialist says we still have the animal instincts that warn us when someone is not on the up-and-up. He says he can't count the times clients who hired him because they'd been mugged said, "I knew something was wrong; I just didn't lis-

ten to my intuition." If the hairs on the back of your neck are
standing up, don't risk your neck. Get the heck out of there.

9. **BE YOUR OWN BODYGUARD.** The time to think about what
you'll do if you're ever attacked is *now*, not when it happens.
Develop a game plan so if you are caught by surprise, you
won't be caught by surprise. If you rehearse your response in
advance, your mind will do what it's been trained to do
instead of going blank.

When traveling solo, pretend you're a security detail for a
VIP (because you are a Very Important Person). Scout the
location. Plan escape routes. Identify hazards. Don't allow
the hotel clerk to announce your room number out loud
when handing you your key. Ask for a room close to the
elevator. You don't have to be paranoid or hyper-vigilant;
just know what you're getting into. Look around first
instead of casually walking up to an ATM to make a deposit.
If it seems all clear, go ahead. If someone loitering nearby
doesn't feel right, take precautions and plan what you would
do if threatened. Maybe you can make that deposit later.
Maybe you can leave your car lights on or take your dog
with you.

Do Not Go Gently into the Not-So-Good Night

> No man can answer for his own valor or courage,
> till he has been in danger.
> —LA ROCHEFOUCAULD

I know from personal experience the importance of keeping
your wits about you when attacked. One beautiful summer
evening, I decided to go for a solo run around our neighborhood. At that time I lived near Pearl Harbor in senior military
housing. I set off just after twilight.

About twenty minutes into my route, I heard someone running up behind me. I thought it was probably a friend coming to join me and didn't look back. The next thing I knew, this person had put a hammerlock around my throat and neck. Thinking this was someone's sick idea of a joke, I choked out, "Hey, that's not funny." This assailant, who was quite a bit taller than me, tightened his grip and I realized this was no friend.

My lifeguard training saved me. I ducked my head and dropped to my knees. This unexpected move and my sudden deadweight surprised the attacker and broke his hold. He clubbed me on the back of the head (which, as my parents could have told you, is the hardest part of my body). Luckily, I had not turned toward him or he would have broken my nose or jaw. Instead, his fist glanced off my skull. I scrambled up and started running and screaming at the same time. At that point, my attacker must have figured I wasn't worth it and hightailed it out of there.

Lifeguards learn not to rear back when someone has us in a choke hold because that exposes our throat even more and cuts off our air supply. Part of lifeguard training was to practice breaking free from someone who has us in a death grip until it became second nature. Even though it had been years since I'd taken those classes, those much-rehearsed release maneuvers kicked in, thank heaven.

I learned a lot from that incident. I learned to stay alert to my surroundings instead of assuming I was safe. I was attacked on a street that was a few hundred yards from an armed guard stationed at the Pacific Fleet Intelligence Center. I was running past houses with open doors no more than fifty feet away—and no one heard a thing. Obviously, this individual was acting impulsively because his behavior did not make any sense. Thankfully, my years of lifesaving training came back to me in that moment of danger and I did the one thing he didn't expect.

Fear Not

Fear is the mother of foresight.
—SIR HENRY TAYLOR

Preparation is the father of safety. Instead of fearing the kinki-
ness of strangers, prepare a game plan so you can handle frightening situations with poise instead of panic. Hopefully, you'll
never encounter a physically threatening bully. However, if you
do, use these tips to increase the likelihood you'll emerge
unscathed.

Action Plan and Discussion Questions

Have you had a dangerous encounter with a stranger? What
happened? What did you do? _____
_____

What will you do if you witness a crime or brutal act? How
will you act quickly and safely to get yourself and other people out of harm's way? _____
_____
_____

What safety measures will you take to minimize the chance
that you'll be endangered by a stranger? _____
_____
_____

Summary

HARMFUL BELIEFS/BEHAVIORS	HELPFUL BELIEFS/BEHAVIORS
Intervene without considering risks *"I can hear the neighbors screaming. I'm going over there."*	Intervene after considering risks *"I don't know them very well. Maybe I should call instead."*
Take safety for granted *"This is a family neighborhood."*	Stay alert and be on guard *"I'm not going to assume anything."*
Go alone *"I can't take this anymore. I'm going over there right now."*	Go with the crowd *"I'm going to ask the couple next door to go with me."*
Try to reason with them *"I'll tell them they're waking up everyone in the neighborhood."*	Trust your instincts *"They sound out of control. The pros need to handle this, not me."*
Act without thinking *"Shut up over there!"*	Plan before acting *"Do I really want to wade into this?"*

Way 23. Continue to Trust, But Tie Your Camel

We have to distrust each other.
It's our only defense against betrayal.
—TENNESSEE WILLIAMS

SURELY HE JESTS. WE DON'T WANT TO DISTRUST EVERYONE, BUT IN our naïveté we don't want to open ourselves to betrayal. Where's the balance?

First, we need to understand that we are most vulnerable when we're caught unaware. A friend learned this the hard way when she took advantage of a free time-share offer. The deal was, she'd get meal vouchers and a two-night stay at an island resort if she'd attend an introductory ninety-minute sales presentation.

Dot signed up and showed up on the appointed weekend. She spent the first day swimming, reading, and kicking back by the pool, and then headed over to the briefing. (She would have been charged full price if she had skipped the sales talk.)

Dot told me, "I had heard these were hard-sell pitches, so I was prepared for their pressure tactics. Sure enough, after the slide presentation, the sales rep started in on us. He used every trick in the book to make us feel obligated to buy a unit. I knew this was part of the deal and I figured sitting through the sales presentation was fair trade for the free weekend.

"What I hadn't counted on was how ruthlessly the sales rep badgered us. He actually targeted two elderly widows in the audience and kept pounding them with these really manipulative questions like 'Don't you love your grandchildren? Wouldn't you like to have a place where you could spend vacations together? You don't know how much more time you have left. Are you going to let your money sit in a bank when you could use it toward building happy memories?'

"One of the staffers noticed my growing distaste for the sales rep's deviousness. She walked over and said, 'You're not going to buy anything, are you?' I looked her straight in the eye and said, 'No way.' She put her hands up in mock surrender and said, 'Come with me, then. You can sign out and leave early.'

"We walked into the office, she closed the door behind me, and we sat down to finish the paperwork. She started chatting me up, and the next thing I knew, she was peppering me with questions about how I could pass up such a good deal. I finally escaped, but not before realizing she had tricked me. I hadn't been vulnerable to their tactics initially because I'd anticipated them. Once I left the room, though, I let my guard down because I thought it was all over, and she tried to take advantage of my weakened defenses."

Most salespeople are ethical individuals who want to satisfy both their needs *and* ours. As Dot learned, though, there are people out there who care only about their agenda. These people see us only as prospects to be sold, quotas to be met, and obstacles to be overcome. If we don't accept this and stay vigilant, we'll be knocked off balance every time it happens.

Believe in Basic Goodness

I was a born pessimist. My first words were,
"My bottle is half empty."
—LACIE HARMON

A woman told me, "This trust issue is a real problem for me. I don't want to go around suspecting that everyone's evil, but I was taken to the cleaners by my own uncle. He showed up in the hospital the very day my husband died and told me that he'd take care of everything. He suggested we move all of my husband's clients over to his management account so I wouldn't have to 'worry' about them. He offered to take care of the books for a while since he knew I had 'more important' things on my mind. In those next few months, he stole thousands of dollars. I couldn't believe a family member would take advantage of a widow with two children. He seemed so solicitous at the time. I never suspected he was out to get our money. I don't know who to believe anymore after I was so wrong about him. It's hard not to be a pessimist after going through something like that."

Have You Been Burned by a Bully?

Whoever battles with monsters had better see that it
does not turn him into a monster.
—FRIEDRICH WILHELM NIETZSCHE

What to do? How can we continue to trust when not everyone is trustworthy? How can we continue to believe in the best of mankind when we've been bested by a bully? The answer to this was explained quite eloquently to me by John Tullius, the founder of the world-renowned Maui Writers Conference. As

I told John of my disillusionment with a bestselling author who turned out to be a cad in person, he paraphrased William Blake's enduring insight about how we can "keep the faith" when someone takes advantage of us. John's interpretation went something like this: "We are all born innocent. At some point, we meet with disillusionment. At that point, we have a choice. We either become cynical skeptics or informed innocents."

Blake's (and John's) timeless insight helped me put my disappointment in its proper perspective. It helped me accept that while there are evil people in the world, there are many more ethical people in the world. One doesn't cancel out the other; the two are not mutually exclusive. The wisest approach to life is to be neither a pessimist or an idealist. It is choosing to be an "informed innocent" who continues to believe the best of people instead of allowing bullies to destroy our faith in the basic goodness of mankind.

Name Their Untrustworthy Game

> It is an equal failing to trust everybody and to trust nobody.
> —THOMAS FULLER

You may be thinking, "Okay, I buy this 'informed innocents' idea. The question remains: What can I do if I'm dealing with someone who turns out to be dishonest?" Hold people accountable for their less-than-honest tactics by saying, "What you're trying to do won't work." Naming a manipulator's game neutralizes it. As soon as Dot recognized the sales rep's unsavory tactics, she could have laughed out loud and said, "Oh, I see what you're doing. You brought me in here so I'd let my guard down, and you're starting up again now that I'm relaxed." The salesperson would have denied it, but Dot's recognition of the strategy would have defeated it.

Add this phrase to your repertoire and trot it out whenever someone tries to manipulate you. You've heard the phrase "Preparation is half the battle"? Preparing with this phrase can keep you *out* of battles. If, in the midst of a negotiation, someone tries to force a false deadline on you, simply say, "I know what you're trying to do and it won't work." Catching them in their act will annul their attack.

What's Your Emotional Achilles' Heel?

If you wake up one morning and you don't have any faults, your address has probably become Forest Lawn.
—VICTORIA MORAN

There is another way you can not be so vulnerable to people out to take advantage of you. Understand that you are not perfect. You see, bullies specifically target our perceived weaknesses. If we are embarrassed about a particular "fault," they will hammer away at it because they know we're sensitive about it.

One man said, "This really helped me understand why my mom would call me selfish whenever I didn't do what she wanted. I never wanted to be perceived as selfish, so whenever she flung that in my face, I'd end up going along with what she wanted." I told him that bullies often project their behavior on us and accuse us of the very thing they're doing. Instead of buying into her ploy, I suggested he think of what other people think about him. His wife, children, and friends all know him to be a kind, caring person. Instead of buying into her manipulative tactic, he should take her accusation on balance and realize it's truer of her than it is of him.

Next time someone tries to take advantage of you, ask yourself, "Is she projecting her behavior on me? Is she saying this because she knows I'm touchy about it? Is what she's saying in line with how other people feel about me?" These questions can give you just the clarity you need to know this denunciation is more reflective of her than it is of you.

Action Plan and Discussion Questions

How are you pessimistic? How are you optimistic? Do you lean toward being jaded or trusting? Explain. _____

_____

_____

What do you think of the concept of being an "informed innocent"? Does it work for you? Why or why not? _____

_____

_____

Can you think of a situation in your personal or professional life where someone tried to take advantage of you? What happened? _____

_____

_____

How are you going to continue being a trusting individual who chooses to see the best in people, instead of becoming a cynic who sees the world as an evil place? _____

_____

_____

What are you going to say if you catch someone trying to manipulate you into going along with what he/she wants?

_____

_____

Summary

HARMFUL BELIEFS/BEHAVIORS	HELPFUL BELIEFS/BEHAVIORS
Vulnerable because we give our blind trust to everyone *"I can't believe she betrayed my confidence."*	Informed innocents who give trust to those who deserve it *"I should have kept those private thoughts to myself."*
Disillusioned when we discover some people are evil *"I'll never feel comfortable sharing intimate details again."*	Understand both evil and beauty exist in our world *"I won't reveal myself on that level until I get to know him better."*
Caught off guard *"I should have realized she had a reason for pressuring me to divulge that."*	Keep on guard *"From now on, I'll know to look out for people who say, 'You can trust me' with that gleam in their eye."*
Not prepared for manipulator's tactics *"I wish I hadn't blurted that out."*	Neutralize manipulative tactics *"What you're trying to do won't work."*

Way 24. Exorcise Your Demons

I like long walks, especially when they are taken
by people who annoy me.
—FRED ALLEN

WHAT ARE YOU DOING WITH THE HURT AND HUMILIATION CAUSED
by dealing with this difficult person? Are you writing in a journal and purging the pain onto pages? If so, good for you.
"Writing out the storm" is a wonderfully tangible way to get
the muck out of your mind.

How else are you exorcising the toxic waste that accumu-
lates as a result of having annoying people in your life? Exorcise
is defined as "to get rid of something troublesome, menacing,
or oppressive; to free yourself from an evil spirit." Wow. This is
exactly what we need to do with the bully in our life.

Run Your Own Life

---

*In the creative action of running I became convinced of my own
importance, certain that my life had significance.*
—Dr. George Sheehan

A friend discovered one of the best ways to exorcise her
demons was to exercise. You've undoubtedly heard this before
and may feel like skipping this part. Please take a few moments
to read it because it will show you how physically working out
is a great way to psychologically work out our stress.

My friend moved from her beloved Hawaii to Atlanta to take
care of her seventy-five-year-old mother who was suffering from
Alzheimer's. She told me, "The day I arrived, I discovered the situation was even worse than I'd anticipated. My brothers had
drained Mom's bank account and allowed her home to fall into a
deplorable state of disrepair. Worse yet, they obviously perceived
me as a threat and tried to take me out of the picture by telling
Mom that the only reason I'd returned was to claim my inheri-
tance. My mom, who was sliding in and out of reality, would
sometimes look at me and ask, 'Did you really come home just to
get my money?' I knew this appalling idea had been planted in
her mind by my brothers, but it didn't make it any less painful."

My friend told me, "I didn't know what to do. I didn't have
any relatives who could intervene, and I'm not sure how much
my mom understood what was happening anyway. I was the
one taking care of her day in and day out, but my brothers had
convinced her that I was trying to put her in a rest home to 'get
her out of the way.' The only thing that kept me sane was going
for long runs."

My friend had actually completed the Ironman Triathlon, a
grueling race on the Big Island of Hawaii that combines a 2.4-
mile swim, a 100+-mile bike ride, and a marathon-length
run—all completed within twenty-four hours. She said, "The

first couple of miles, I'd be 'in my head' replaying what was happening. Then I'd get back in my body, start noticing my surroundings, and my anger would rush out of me like water from a broken wading pool. I could actually feel my consciousness expanding back out into the world instead of banging around in my brain. By the end of a run, I would have realized that as horrible as this situation was, there were still things in my life to be grateful for."

Do Sweat It

> Sadness is almost never anything but a form of fatigue.
> —ANDRÉ GIDE

You've probably heard the phrase "Don't sweat it." Forget that. *Do* sweat it. Sweat occurs when we exercise aerobically at a level that causes our heart to beat at 60 percent or more of its maximum, which oxygenates the brain and body and deepens our breathing. Research shows that breathing deeply is one of the best ways to release stored tension. Furthermore, aerobic exercise gets us out of our head (which is either swirling with anger or swamped with despair) and into our gut (which is how we regain our center). Sweating helps us excrete toxic emotions and replenishes the energy that's been drained by our bouts with bullies.

The bully's MO (modus operandi) is to break our spirit (our life force) because he or she knows we won't offer any opposition if we're emotionally exhausted. Think about it. If you're dealing with a bully right now, what is your mental and physical state? Do you feel depressed? Do you feel like no matter what you do, you can't win? Do you understand this is how bullies keep you in their clutches? They wear you down so you won't be up to the task of taking them on. Bullies want us to feel beat before we even start, so we don't start.

That's why it's imperative to become physically active. As

long as we remain lethargic and sedentary, it will be impossible to reverse the situation because challenging bullies requires energy we don't have.

Move It to Lose It

> A person is really alive only when he is moving forward
> to something more.
> —WINFRED RHOADES

A man approached me after a seminar and said, "I have to tell you the ten minutes we spent on 'Move It to Lose It' was worth the price of admission. When I married my wife, I was an athlete. That was my identity. I grew up in the mountains and was always outdoors doing something from the time I was seven years old. That all changed after a couple of years of marriage. At first I just thought my wife was jealous of the time I spent on sports because she wanted me to spend more time with her. She wasn't the outdoorsy type and always grumbled when I set off for a day outside with my friends.

"Over time, she became more and more vocal about her disdain for athletes. We'd pass people running on the highway and she'd make some caustic remark about how 'vain and selfish' they were and how they must be single because married people with responsibilities didn't have time to indulge in such hedonistic activities.

"I started cutting back on my hobbies because I wanted my marriage to work and I thought that meant compromising. I bought into her accusations that I was being selfish and that I valued my friends more than I did her. It got to the point where I would go for weeks without doing anything outside. My friends kept telling me I was whipped, but I never saw it.

"I realize now that it wasn't just that she didn't share that part of my life. She was scared I'd meet someone else who loved sports, and I'd leave her. I don't know whether it was on a conscious or unconscious level, but she did everything in her power to destroy that side of me."

He shook his head ruefully, "After five years of this blah life, I didn't even recognize the guy looking back at me in the mirror. I got to the point where I didn't care if it was selfish; I just knew I couldn't live the rest of my life like this. In a kind of sick way, I realized my wife liked me fat and unhappy because it kept me home—kind of a male 'barefoot and pregnant' thing. If I ever get married again, it's going to be to someone who likes being active instead of to someone who tries to make me feel like a terrible person for doing something I love."

What and Who Do You Love?

> Don't move, I want to forget you just the way you are.
> —HENNY YOUNGMAN

This man's story is important for several reasons. Bullies don't want us to move forward with our lives, they want to keep us where we are—with them. They do their best to prevent us from spending time in activities we love and with people we love for several reasons. Joy is defined as "the emotion evoked by well-being, success, good fortune" and the "prospect of possessing what one desires."

Bullies see activities and people that bring us joy as competition. They do their darndest to break our bonds to buddies and hobble our involvement in hobbies because they don't want us doing anything that:

- strengthens our sense of self and lessens their control over us
- gives us a sense of success, which makes them superfluous
- makes us happy and causes us to realize how unhappy we are with them

- brings us into contact with people who notice our decline and warn us against the bully

This is like a triple whammy. Bullies deprive us of our friends and family (our support network), of the hobbies we love (our identity and source of well-being), and of physical activity (the wellspring of vigor)—so we become inert and stay in the relationship. Their strategy is to de-spirit us so we simply don't have the strength necessary to break free. That is why it is imperative that you start:

- spending time with friends and loved ones
- reinvolving yourself in hobbies that give you a sense of joy
- engaging in aerobic activity a minimum of three times a week so you build the fitness that gives you the physical and psychological fortitude to resist a bully's efforts to bend you to his or her will

From Enervated to Energetic

> The soul of walking is liberty, perfect liberty, to think, feel,
> do just as one pleases.
> —WILLIAM HAZLITT

You may be thinking, "I don't have the time or energy to exercise. I'm so busy or tired, it's all I can do to get through the day." That's understandable. Do you realize, though, that if you're waiting for the time and energy to exercise, they will never show up? Do you know of any people with spare time on their hands? Do you understand that lethargy is a result of *no* exercise, not a reason to avoid exercise?

Do you understand walking or working out is a form of liberty? It's a way to free yourself from the hold of a bully who is trying to rob you of your independence and lock you up spiritually, emotionally, and physically.

As long as you stay sedentary, you will stay trapped. You'll be trapped by your own unwillingness to do the one thing that will give you the wherewithal to change your situation. All the good intentions in the world mean nothing if you don't have the inner resources to carry out your determination. That's what energy is, the means to activate intentions. Energy is defined as "the capacity of acting or being alive." Enervate is defined as "lacking physical, mental, or moral vigor."

Bullies win if they succeed in enervating you (lessening your strength and vitality so you lack vigor). One of the ways to win our battle with bullies is to take responsibility for reversing the vigor mortis they cause with their incessant demands and demeans.

Reverse Vigor Mortis

Half the spiritual difficulties that men and women suffer
arise from a morbid state of health.
—HENRY WARD BEECHER

The question isn't whether you have the time or energy to exercise. The question is, Do you want a better life? Do you want to feel strong again? Do you want to take control of who you are? If you do, get a move on today. Movement cures morbidity. Moving your body supplies you with vigor so you have the strength to counter a bully's attempts to sap your inner resources.

Be sure to team up with a buddy for your daily walk, workout, or sport. It's the key to sustaining good intentions because it makes exercising more fun and helps us keep our commitment to show up. Finding an exercise partner is especially important when battling a bully because s/he is going to do everything in his or her power to sabotage your attempts to get fit.

Bullies See Fitness as a Threat

> I take care of me. I'm the only one I've got.
> —GROUCHO MARX

Bullies may see your efforts to become physically active as a direct threat to their supremacy and may resort to scurrilous tactics to derail your determination to improve yourself. They may call you names, say it costs too much, or takes up too much time. They may accuse you of being frivolous and "putting your vanity first" instead of taking care of the kids, the chores, or them. They may tempt you with alternatives (sleeping in, dates) to keep you at home with them.

Maintain clarity that getting and staying healthy is your right. Keep your touchstone with you to remind yourself that you're not going to allow anyone to undermine your resolve to restore vigor. Picture the Rights/Needs Seesaw and see that you are a samurai who is taking care of yourself, and that any attempt to keep you from being active is just another attempt to keep you downtrodden. Understand that confidence comes from being vital, and you have the power to make that happen starting today if you start dedicating thirty minutes a day to being physically active.

Tyrants Will Try to Put Down Your Uprising

> How many therapists does it take to change a lightbulb?
> One, but the lightbulb's really got to *want* to change.
> —INTERNET JOKE

Resolve to change the status quo, even though the bully in your life won't want you to. As the saying goes, "Who ya gonna call?" Are you going to call that neighbor who's told you before that she wishes she had the discipline to get up early in the morning and walk? Are you going to call a friend who once expressed interest in a dance class? Are you going to call your local community center and sign up for that karate class? Your future is a phone call away. Make it now.

Action Plan and Discussion Questions

Are you physically active? If so, what do you do and how often? _____

_____

Do you feel depressed or lethargic? Why do you think your energy is low? _____

_____

_____

Is there a person in your life who is sapping your strength? Who is this person and what is he or she doing? _____

_____

_____

What physical activity could you do to excrete toxins, replenish your energy, and rebuild strength? When, where, and how often are you going to do this? _____

_____

_____

What is a hobby you love to do that could bring joy back into your life? When, where, and how often are you going to do this? _____

_____

_____

Summary

HARMFUL BELIEFS/BEHAVIORS	HELPFUL BELIEFS/BEHAVIORS
Don't sweat it *"I know I should go to the gym, but it's the last thing I feel like doing."*	Do sweat it *"Exercising is the last thing I want to do, which means it's exactly what I ought to do."*
Feeling down and resigned *"I can barely get through the day. I just don't have any fight left in me."*	Feeling up to the task (master) *"I've got to get back to my old self. Who is that stranger in the mirror?"*
Sedentary and isolated *"Well, another 'exciting' weekend where the most interesting thing I did was pick up the mail."*	Social and actively involved *"I'm going to check out that water aerobics class Saturday morning. I heard some neighbors talking about it, and they go every week."*
Deprives you of friends, family, fitness, and fun *"Why do you always give me such a hard time for wanting to visit my sister?"*	Determined to keep friends, family, fitness, and fun *"I'm meeting my sister in New York this weekend. We're going gallery-hopping in SoHo."*

Way 25. Lean on We

Instead of loving your enemies,
treat your friends a little better.
—ED HOWER

"I DON'T KNOW IF I COULD HAVE SURVIVED THESE LAST FEW months if it hadn't been for friends," one woman told me. "You know the phrase 'They were there for me'? Well, my friends were everywhere for me.

"I've worked as a secretary at our local university for the last four years. I've always enjoyed my work and I get along well—well, I used to get along well—with the students and faculty. That all fell apart earlier this year when a new dean was hired for our department. I don't know how this man got the job, but he probably schmoozed the hiring committee with his smooth-operator act. He started coming on to me the first week he was in our office—not overtly in a way he could be caught, but in subtle, double entendre ways that left me feeling slimy.

"I was working late one night, and he walked up behind me, leaned over the back of my chair, and pretended to look at what I was writing while trying to sneak a peek down my blouse. I turned and said, 'What are you doing?' He gave one of his sick grins and said, 'Just enjoying the view.'

"That did it. I pushed my chair back, gathered my things, and left. Or at least I tried to leave. He blocked the door and said, 'Come on, don't be so uptight.' I pushed him aside, ran out of the building, and filed a grievance against him the next morning.

"The next day I was called into the main office. I entered the room ready to report what had been happening over the past few months. I never had a chance. The *dean* had filed a grievance against *me*! I sat there in shock as the administrative officer read his complaint against me. In essence, the dean said I had come on to him and he felt he had no choice but to report my 'infatuation' out of self-protection.

"I tried to explain that the dean was the one who ought to be called on the carpet, but I could see that as far as the admin officer was concerned, it was a 'he said, she said' situation. I was put on probation and told I would be terminated if there were any other reports of this kind of harassment.

"I can't put into words how I felt. It was incomprehensible to me that someone would out and out lie the way he did and get away with it. It was even more incomprehensible that *I* would end up in trouble when he was responsible for the whole thing. I approached several secretaries and asked if they would testify on my behalf. They all said they felt bad about what I was going through, but weren't willing to jeopardize their jobs because they were afraid he would turn on them, too.

"Thank heaven for my friends. I spent hours on the phone pouring out my frustration. They were so patient. I'm sure there were times they had better things to do than hear the latest chapter in my battle with the school—but I guess they realized they were the only ones I could turn to.'"

Repeat After Me, "I Am NOT Crazy"

Feeling crazy may be a mark of sanity in some situations.
—ANNE WILSON SCHAEF

Do you have friends to turn to if someone's turned on you? Friends can be your saving grace if you're unlucky enough to find yourself in a nightmarish situation. Friends can reassure you that you're not crazy and you're not alone.

This is especially important because bullies tell us repeatedly that *we're* crazy. Their intent is to make us doubt our sanity so we're more susceptible to their propaganda. Many interviewees told me they felt like they were losing their mind—because the bully in their life kept telling them they were.

One woman gave up her business and flew to another country to live with a man she'd worked with in the foreign service. This woman had been a successful entrepreneur who had started and sold a million-dollar company. Within a few months of arriving, she was a complete wreck. This man would tell her to schedule dinner plans and then deny ever saying that. He belittled her constantly with "Can't you do anything right?" On the way to social occasions, he would deliberately pick a fight and then sweep through the door, the charming hail-fellow-well-met, while apologizing for his partner, who was a "basket case." He kept saying, "You are some crazy broad." After months of his relentless attacks, this formerly confident woman started wondering if she was.

Don't Purchase the Propaganda

> Keep reading between the lies.
> —GOODMAN ACE

Propaganda is defined as "ideas or allegations spread deliberately to further one's cause or to damage an opposing cause."
Propaganda is a bully's stock-in-trade.

Terrorists and cultists know that repeatedly bombarding
someone with one-sided information in a vacuum of opposition eventually results in that individual adopting the partisan
beliefs. Cult leaders deliberately subject recruits to around-the-
clock indoctrination and cut off all contact with loved ones so
recruits are out of touch with reality. They take advantage of
the recruits' vulnerable, isolated, sleepless status to imprint the
desired beliefs.

Bullies do much the same thing. They subject us to round-
the-clock indoctrination. They try to isolate us by keeping us
apart from loved ones. They knock us off balance by behaving
in contradictory ways that make us think we've lost touch with
reality. They tell us over and over, in our vulnerable state and in
a vacuum of input to the contrary, that we're nuts. After a
while, we feel like we've lost our mind, and we have. The bully
has stolen it. It's in his or her possession.

Aldous Huxley knew about the insidious effects of brain-
washing. He said, "If the emotions of fear, rage, or anxiety are
kept at a high pitch of intensity for a long enough time, the
brain goes 'on strike.' When this happens, new behavior patterns may be installed with the greatest of ease."

So what to do? Don't go it alone. If you lose touch with
your friends, you'll lose touch with reality. Your friends will
keep you sane because they'll assure you that you are sane. They
will give you balanced input so you can put thoughts in perspective. They'll help you see that it's not you who's unstable,

it's the bully, who is deliberately undermining you in an effort to make you lose yourself.

Seek Friends in Deed When in Need

> In prosperity our friends know us; in adversity
> we know our friends.
> —JOHN COLLINS, BRITISH CRITIC

For all the reasons we've previously covered, it can be a daunting task to take on a tyrant. Most of us have no desire to destroy a fellow human being and we're devastated that someone's trying to do it to us. Furthermore, it's hard to match the obsessive zeal of a bully who's doing his or her best to debilitate us.

Leaning on friends is a way of tapping into their strength so we don't have to supply all our own. My favorite teacher used to say, "Encouragement is oxygen to the soul." When our energy tank is drained, we can fill 'er up with the encouragement of people who care. Perhaps most important, frequent contact with friends can render propaganda meaningless because we'll know it's not true.

It is now you and your friends against the bully—which makes you more formidable. If you're intimidated at the prospect of calling a support group, please know you'll be in safe hands and hearts. You don't need to take my word for this. Take the word of an extremely successful broker who discovered this for herself.

I had the privilege of speaking at a conference for some of the country's most successful female financial advisers. At a dinner one evening, we went around the table and shared how we'd gotten into the business. Every woman had a fascinating, against-all-odds story of how she'd made her mark in this mostly male enclave. We were all particularly impressed with one woman's story.

This now successful executive had sought a divorce from a vindictive husband years ago. Much to her dismay, he succeeded in getting custody of their three young sons when, as she said, "the only women in the South who didn't get custody of their children were drug addicts or prostitutes. Or," as she added ruefully, "uppity women who dared to divorce their powerful attorney husband."

Get By with a Little Help from Your Friends

> Friends are God's apology for relatives.
> —HUGH KINGSMILL, BRITISH WRITER

Voice trembling at the memory of that horrible time, she said she went to Displaced Homemakers—the last place she, a formerly affluent woman, ever thought she'd end up. She took a placement test and was told she either needed to own her own company or be president. Her counselor suggested she call a broker in town, express interest in his profession, and ask if she could interview him over lunch. The broker agreed. During their meal, he said he loved his job because he was in control of his outcome and his income and he felt his work mattered and made a positive difference for others. She was sold. This now prosperous financial adviser (who's since reconnected with her sons) said she never would have had the insight or courage to make that call if it hadn't been for the support she received from Displaced Homemakers.

Could I Have a Little Support?

> When one's own problems are unsolvable and all best efforts are frustrated, it is lifesaving to listen to other people's problems.
> —SUZANNE MASSIE

If for whatever reason you feel you have no one to turn to, rest assured. There are support groups designed for people just like you. You are going to feel such relief when you contact these groups because they will believe you. They will understand your story because they have heard it before. They may not have heard your specific tale, but there are patterns to bully behavior and they have heard every variation. They will embrace you and support you through this mess. Many of the people supervising these groups have "been there, done that," and they have dedicated themselves to helping others as they themselves were once helped.

Action Plan and Discussion Questions

Has the bully in your life tried to cut you off from friends and family? If so, explain. _____
_____
_____

Have you been going it alone? Could you benefit from leaning on we? Name a couple of friends you've lost touch with. How are you going to reconnect with them? _____
_____
_____

Has a bully in your life been showering you with propaganda? What has he or she been saying to you? Have you started believing this indoctrination? How so? _____
_____
_____

Please refer to the Resource Directory in the back of this book and find a support group you're going to contact. Which one did you choose? When are you going to call them? _____
_____
_____

Summary

HARMFUL BELIEFS/BEHAVIORS	HELPFUL BELIEFS/BEHAVIORS
Bully isolates us from friends *"I haven't seen my family in months. I miss them."*	We reach out to friends *"I'm going to visit my family this weekend."*
We lose touch with reality *"He keeps telling me no one likes me. Maybe he's right."*	We stay in touch with reality *"I'm giving Tina a call. She'll give me an honest response."*
Bully indoctrinates us with propaganda to weaken us *"He says that people laugh at me behind my back."*	We stay strong by not buying into intentional indoctrination *"I've known these people for twenty years, and he can't make me doubt them."*
We feel all alone *"No one would believe me if I told them how awful it's been."*	We seek out support *"I'm going to call the shelter. They'll understand what I've been going through."*

Way 26. Give Schoolyard Bullies an Education

School is about two parts ABCs to fifty parts "Where Do I
Stand in the Great Pecking Order of Humankind."
—BARBARA KINGSOLVER

THIS HAS BEEN AN EXTREMELY CHALLENGING CHAPTER TO WRITE
because there initially seemed to be few viable answers to the
question "How can you stop a bully from picking on you at
school?" If it's been hard for me to write, imagine what it's like
to live.

A vanload of teenage boys told me, "Mrs. Horn, the advice
adults give us about bullies is a joke. They tell us, 'If someone
picks on you, just walk away.' Right!" they snorted. "If we
walk away, the bully will come after us. Parents tell us, 'Report
bullies to your teacher.'" They all snorted again. "If we tell
teachers what happened, they say they can't do anything
because they didn't see it. If bullies *do* get in trouble, they get
suspended—which is what they want anyway."

Are the boys giving me this report from an inner city school
where gangs are the norm? No, they attend a public school in a
county that is often lauded as one of the finest academic school
districts in the country. This school boasts a record-breaking

high school miler, extracurricular activities galore, and many National Honor Society members. It also has an everyday threat of bullying that almost every other school-aged child in our country has to face Monday through Friday.

A study by the National Association of School Psychologists done in the fall of 2000 reported that more than 160,000 children a day skip school because they fear bullies. A National Institutes of Health study released in the *Journal of the American Medical Association* reveals that almost a third of sixth to tenth graders—5.7 million children nationwide—have experienced some kind of bullying. "A lot of kids have grief, loss, pain, and it's unresolved," the study said. What can we do?

Convince Bullies to Leave You Alone

To a child that is picked on, having a good friend,
being accepted for what you are, or just simply
being left alone would be like a dream.
—"THE BROKEN TOY"

One of the first things we can do is to stop handing our kids meaningless platitudes that minimize their trauma and give them the impression we don't understand what they're going through. When kids hear the clichéd advice, "Bullies bother you to get attention. Ignore them and they'll leave you alone," they feel like no one is really listening.

Many articles on this subject and in-school programs suggest that kids befriend the bully. This "remove the thorn from the misunderstood lion's paw and he'll become the lamb's friend" idea works . . . occasionally. However, as my friend Mary Loverde says, "You can remove the thorn from the lion's paw, but he's still a lion, and when he gets hungry, you're lunch!"

Are You a Lamb or a Lion?

> The lion and the lamb may lie down together,
> but the lamb won't get much sleep.
> —WOODY ALLEN

Mary, author of *I Used to Have a Handle on Life, but it Broke,* pegged it. "We'd love to believe that love will prevail and that if we don't bother a bully, he or she won't bother us." In the real world, kids jockey for position. As Barbara Kingsolver so astutely observed, adolescence is a time when kids are establishing where they are in the great pecking order of life. We may wish this weren't so, but children constantly size each other up to figure out who's the alpha dog. Trying to ignore a bully invites aggression because it is perceived as avoidance.

I've come to the conclusion that we do children a disservice when we give them the impression that their only and best option is to stay away from bullies. That's just not realistic. Telling children to stay away from someone who's mistreating them gives bullies continued power and relegates your son or daughter to living in fear. I think it is far better to teach children how to take care of themselves so they can deal with aggressors instead of hide from them.

You may agree with this in theory. The question is, how can children deal with bullies without putting themselves at risk? One way is to become a cool cat.

Adopt Your Cat's Courage

A cat who doesn't run is no fun.
—MURPH, SAM HORN'S DOG

Do you have a cat and a dog at home? Have you ever noticed how your cat usually rules the roost, even if your dog is the larger, stronger animal? Look at what happens when your dog approaches. Your cat usually arches her back, puffs up, and glares menacingly at the dog. If your cat holds her ground, your dog will often back off and not bother her because she has such a "paws off" presence.

I see this played out every day I walk my dog Murph. We have several cats on our street. One, Mr. Gray Cat, has an imperial presence. When he sees Murph coming, he—there's no other word for it—*expands*. He puffs himself up, stands his ground, and glares at Murph. Murph gives him a wide berth because he exudes a "Don't even think about it" attitude.

On the other hand, there's a calico cat who panics as soon as she sees us and takes off running. Murph is at the end of her leash straining to get at her. Hmmm. Two different cats, two different attitudes, two different outcomes.

I think kids need to adopt the attitude of Mr. Gray Cat when dealing with a kid who's trying to establish him- or herself as top dog. Tell them to picture how your cat can back down a dog three times her size simply by standing her ground and sending out a "Don't even think about it" attitude. Standing your ground is such an important concept. A child trying to walk away from a bully will often have the same effect as a cat trying to slink away from a dog. Cats know not to show fear or the dog will be after them in a second. Most dogs would win a battle with a cat if they tried, but they *don't* try when they can tell the cat will defend itself.

Be a Cool Cat

You may not be interested in war, but war is interested in you.
—Leo Tolstoy

Most children are not interested in bullying others. Unfortunately, there are probably children who are interested in bullying them. At the dinner table tonight, talk about this cat-dog scenario. Ask your kids to picture the difference between a scaredy cat and a cool cat. Suggest that from now on they might want to act like a cool cat if someone starts picking on them. Stand in front of a mirror and ask them to adopt the pose of a scaredy cat. They'll probably duck their head, hunch their shoulders, and look like they're ready to flee. Now ask them to pull themselves up to their full height and project a "Don't even think about bothering me" look. The following are just a few of the ways they can look like a cool cat.

SCAREDY CAT	COOL CAT
Run and hide	Stand your ground
Shrink back	Puff up
Slouch, hunch shoulders	Pull self up to full height
Eyes darting, looking down or away	Eyes open and locked on
"Don't hurt me" attitude	"Don't mess with me" attitude
Show fear	Show courage

Now Is the Time for All Good People to Come to Their Own . . . Self-Defense

> At the bottom of every one of your fears is the fear that
> you can't handle whatever life may bring you.
> —SUSAN JEFFERS

You may be wondering, "Aren't there more tangible ways for my kids to protect themselves if they're being picked on?" Matter of fact, yes. While I was being prepped for an appearance on the TV program *To Tell the Truth* (what fun), I noticed a photo on the makeup artist's mirror of him and his son receiving their black belts in karate. I asked about it and he told me how this had come about. His son had been the smallest kid in his class, and as a result, he got pushed around a lot. The father said, "In the beginning, I told him to mind his own business, but realized what useless advice that was when he told me, 'Dad, I tried to ignore them, but it doesn't work. Who likes to be ignored?' That's when I realized bullies who are ignored escalate their behavior so we're forced to pay attention to them. I decided to sign us both up for martial arts classes. Within weeks, I noticed a change. My son held himself differently and projected a confidence that just hadn't been there before. After that, it didn't matter that my son was still one of the smallest kids in school. Tough guys leave him alone because they know he can take care of himself."

Do your children know how to take care of themselves? Registering your children and yourself in a self-defense or martial arts course is a good investment in bully prevention. Hopefully, you'll never have to use the skills you learn in class (unless you choose to compete in contests). However, the physical assurance you gain from knowing how to neutralize attacks will persuade most bullies to walk on by. Your "cool cat" confidence changes the risk-benefit ratio because you no longer look like easy prey. As this father said, "My son may not be able to stop bullies from hassling everybody. He can stop them from hassling *him*."

Another way we can help children achieve a cat-like confidence is to role-play scenarios in which they stand up to bullies instead of run from them.

Turn Learned Helplessness into Acquired Courage

It is terribly easy to shake a man's faith in himself. To take advantage of that, to break a man's spirit is the devil's work.
—GEORGE BERNARD SHAW

Learned helplessness is a psychological term that describes the dispirited mental state that results from being repeatedly put in situations in which we feel powerless. Anxiety is defined as "not knowing." Most of us have never been taught how to deal with someone who is threatening us. Since we don't know what to do or say to make bullies leave us alone, we feel helpless around them. This makes matters worse because bullies sense our fear and are emboldened by it.

Furthermore, confidence is defined in two words: "I can." Think about it. If you have a high level of competence in something, you feel confident in that situation. Most of us don't feel we're good at handling bullies. This lack of know-how makes us even more afraid, which encourages more aggression.

What to do? Children can counteract this feeling of hopelessness and helplessness by practicing situations in which they respond competently to a bully's attack. By rehearsing scenarios in which they think and act confident, they know what to do the next time someone tries to bully them.

This weekend, take your children aside and tell them you're going to play a game. You're going to pretend to be a bully so they can practice standing up for themselves. Let your child know you're going to say mean things so they can practice coming back with "cool cat" responses. Ask which remarks bother them so you can prepare them for the real thing. Throughout the weekend, say "Here comes the bully," which is your password for this game. Then walk up and say something like "Hey, shrimp, give me your sandwich." They can rehearse puffing up and saying something like "Oh, go pick on someone who's not half your size."

Brainstorm responses that work so they have a repertoire of remarks that will convince bullies to take it somewhere else. Role-playing desensitizes them so they're no longer taken aback (look at the significance of those words) by taunts. The next time a bully challenges them, they will have "been there, practiced this," so they'll be able to think on their feet instead of being struck dumb.

Believe You Are Brave, Inside and Out

> I went to a really tough school. We wrote essays on
> what we wanted to be *if* we grew up.
> —LENNY BRUCE

There's another way to help children bully-proof themselves. Fellow author Victoria Moran told me a wonderful story about a famous actress she was privileged to meet. Victoria was interviewing the woman for her book *Lit from Within*, which discusses how we can be beautiful inside and out. Victoria was intrigued with this woman's style and wanted to know how she had acquired the reputation of being a room-stopper, the type of person everyone looks at admiringly when she walks in because she has such commanding presence. The woman confessed, "I'm not really beautiful. I realized a long time ago that life would be better if I was, so I *decided* to be beautiful, and people have believed it ever since."

Life will be better if children decide to be brave. Once they believe they are brave, other children will believe it, too. Children who have been targeted by a bully spend a lot of time thinking about what the bully has done to them and worrying about what the bully will do to them. Focusing on these frightening images causes them to be filled with dread—the opposite of determination. The good news is, they can counteract this by filling their minds with images of confidence.

You Can Beat the Giants

Whatever kind of look you were going for, you missed.
—T-SHIRT SLOGAN

If kids want to look and feel brave, they need to start telling themselves they're brave. Suggest that every time they're in front of a mirror at home, they look themselves in the eye and say, "I am brave. I am brave. I am brave." Post signs with I AM BRAVE in places (inside a notebook, on their personal computer, by their desk or bed) where they'll see this affirmation throughout the day.

This may sound like pop psychology, but it works. A fact of human behavior is that we act in accordance with our beliefs, and we believe what we repeatedly hear, think, and tell ourselves. If we replace cowardly "I'm scared" messages with confident "I'm brave" messages, the brain will accept what we tell it and our body will behave accordingly.

This was delightfully demonstrated by a story told me by a successful executive. I had asked how he got his confidence and positive attitude, and he said, "I owe it all to my mom. She read the book *The Magic of Believing*, and it changed her life.

"Our small-town Little League team won our local championship, so we advanced to the regional tournament, where our first-round opponent was the top-seeded Giants. The Giants were just that. They were all five to six inches taller than us and at least fifty pounds heavier.

"No one thought we stood a chance except my mom. She plastered posters all over our house that said 'Beat the Giants!' 'You Can Win.' My friends came over and saw them and teased me unmercifully. I was so embarrassed.

"But guess what? We beat the Giants! Thanks to my mom, I learned early in life that you can do what you want if you just believe in it hard enough."

Are Your Kids Getting Emotionally Mugged?

> A liberal is a conservative who's been mugged.
> —ANONYMOUS

You may not agree with these suggestions to be a cool cat, stand your ground, learn martial arts or self-defense, or believe yourself to be brave and I understand your reticence to recommend anything that might put your children at risk. The problem is, they're at risk whether we want them to be or not, and it's up to us to teach them and prepare them how they can handle bullies so they can take care of themselves.

Whatever you do, be sure to sit down with your kids and discuss this all-important issue. Start off by asking questions instead of giving advice. Find out what *they* think, what *they've* been dealing with. Ask if their school has zero tolerance and what happens if they defend themselves from someone who is pushing them around. Brainstorm options about how they can protect themselves from troublemakers. Clarify whether they have permission to stick up for themselves if they're being picked on, and what such behavior looks like.

Whatever you do, please understand that doing nothing about this problem does *not* make it go away, it makes it worse. Give your children a fighting chance by preparing them to deal with intimidators so they feel powerful instead of powerless.

Action Plan and Discussion Questions

Were you bullied as a child? How old were you? What happened? _____

_____

_____

_____

Do you have or know children who are being bullied? What has been your advice to them? Has it worked? Why or why not? _____

_____

_____

_____

What are you going to suggest to them now? Are you going to recommend they puff up like a cat and see themselves holding their ground? Explain. _____

_____

_____

_____

Do your local schools have a character-development program in place? If so, describe its impact on students. _____

_____

_____

_____

What type of disciplinary program does your local school have for problem behavior? Does it work to deter bully behavior? What type of program would you like to lobby for? _____

_____

_____

_____

Do you believe there is value in training ourselves in martial arts? What are you going to do to help you and your children grow more confident in your ability to defend yourselves? _____

_____

_____

_____

Summary

HARMFUL BELIEFS/BEHAVIORS	HELPFUL BELIEFS/BEHAVIORS
Parental advice to kids is idealistic *"Just ignore him and he'll go away."*	Make advice to kids realistic *"Walk tall and exude confidence and he'll probably pass you by."*
Beat up the bully *"I'm going to haul off and let him have it. I don't care if I get in trouble."*	Befriend the bully *"Josh, come be on our team. We need someone who can rebound and get the ball down the court."*

Physical weakness invites bullying
"Maybe if I take this back hallway, Josh won't find me. Oh, no, he saw me."

Bullies like to be top dog
"I'm not doing anything to you. Why are you picking on me?"

Run and hide from bullies
"I'll stay in class instead of going out on the playground."

Physical assurance prevents bullying
"I feel I can handle anything and anyone, thanks to those judo classes."

Puff up like a cat
"I'm going to hold my ground and back this bully down."

Role-play standing up to bullies
"Give the ball back now, Josh."

Way 27. Speak No Evil: Hate Is Not an Option

"You despise me, don't you?"
"Well, if I gave it any thought, I would."
—HUMPHREY BOGART'S RESPONSE IN THE MOVIE *CASABLANCA*

DON'T GIVE ANY THOUGHT TO DESPISING PEOPLE. AS MENTIONED before, it's okay to be angry with a bully; it's just not okay for that anger to metastasize into hate or vengeance.

Speaking poorly of other people—no matter how they deserve it—only reflects poorly on us. Even if listeners agree with our assessment of this individual, at some level they're wondering, "I wonder what s/he says about me when *I'm* not around?!" Bad-mouthing bullies doesn't improve the situation or their behavior, it only compromises our peace of mind and other people's perception of us.

Upon hearing this idea, a seminar attendee protested, "I thought you told us silence sanctions." I clarified: "I'm not suggesting we *accept* a bully's behavior, I'm suggesting it's counterproductive to go around telling everyone what a slimeball this person is."

Don't Bad-Mouth Bullies

> They say you shouldn't say nothing about the dead
> unless it's good. He's dead. Good.
> —MOMS MABLEY, AMERICAN COMEDIENNE

"This was one of the hardest aspects of this whole nightmare," confessed the financial adviser whose attorney husband had taken her children away from her and then added insult to injury by stashing them in boarding school.

"When I visited them on weekends, everything in me wanted to set the record straight. I yearned to tell them I wasn't the one responsible for the whole mess—their father was. He was telling them terrible things about me, and I desperately wanted them to hear my side of the story. He told them I had driven us into bankruptcy, which was a total fabrication. I tried to explain to the kids that he was the one who ran up our credit card bills and drove us into debt. My ten-year-old son looked me in the eyes and said, 'Mom, Dad says one thing and you say another. I don't know who to believe anymore, so I don't believe either one of you.'

"Hearing that broke my heart. It was especially painful because I always tried to be honest and behave with integrity. To hear my own son tell me he didn't trust me anymore was devastating. I decided at that moment that what my kids needed more than the truth was one parent who was acting like a responsible adult. They didn't need to be put in the middle of what was going on between their father and me. They already had one parent who was saturating them with vindictiveness; they didn't need their other parent doing the same thing. My therapist kept telling me, 'They'll figure it out on their own. You have to trust that refusing to stoop to your husband's level is the best thing you can do for them right now.'

"Her advice offered little consolation at the time. Hoping

that my sons would eventually learn the truth and know who I was offered little comfort. What if it never happened? What if they had been so poisoned against me they never gave me a second chance? I can hardly express what it was like imagining that this could happen. However, the alternative of trashing their dad and driving my sons deeper into this universal skepticism was not an option. Thankfully, my therapist's prediction materialized and my sons and I are closer than ever now."

I Hate When That Happens

> Hating people is like burning down your own
> house to get rid of a rat.
> —HARRY EMERSON FOSDICK

One woman said, "I agree with this in theory, but it's hard to do—especially if someone has ruined my reputation, cost me my job, and made my life hell."

I'm not saying it's easy. I'm saying it's necessary if we're to move on and not let the bully "win." Get clear that the bully *does* win if we seethe with resentment and become hate-filled. Choosing not to become bitter is one of the few things we can control about what's happened to us. How do we pull this off? Surrounding ourselves with friends, exorcising our demons, and engaging in joyful activities are all tangible ways to counterbalance the dark forces in our life.

Another way to not allow this person to drag you down to his or her level is to get absolutely clear that you will continue to be the quality of person you want to be—even though the other person isn't.

Beauty and the Beast

Everything is beautiful at the ballet.
—*A Chorus Line*

This line from the Tony Award–winning play *A Chorus Line* is sung by a character who escapes her hard life by going to the ballet. It's her way of sinking into the delight of dancing instead of sinking into despair.

She's right. We can counteract the temptation to "switch to the dark side" (think *Star Wars*) by deliberately bringing beauty into our life. Simply said, it's hard to be bitter when we're surrounded by beauty.

When I was in the midst of my trial by fire, I was lucky enough to be renting a house that had a yard full of roses. Seeing my sons off to school and then watering and pruning those rosebushes became my morning ritual. How peaceful it was to spend those few minutes in the early morning air lovingly tending those healthy plants. Every morning I'd clip a few just-right buds and display them around the house in colorful vases. I always placed a fresh rose by my computer where I could look at it during the day. My mind was nourished by these colorful gifts from nature. They would nurture my spirit and offer tangible reminders that while there are beasts in the world, there is also beauty.

Earthly Pleasures Counteract Evil

*In this silent, serene wilderness the weary can gain
a heart-bath in perfect peace.*
—JOHN MUIR

A man who had been fired by a bully boss because he had dared to challenge him said, "I spent the first week after being told to clear out my desk pacing back and forth in our house thinking of all the ways I could retaliate against this guy. I was so wired I couldn't go to sleep at night. I'd lie there staring at the ceiling, hatching vengeful, get-even plots. The second week, my wife handed me a trowel and wisely told me to take my anger out on our garden.

"That's what I did. I went to Home Depot, bought just about everything in sight, and spent every morning that next week on my hands and knees weeding, terracing, planting, and watering. In retrospect, it was one of the most therapeutic things I could have done for myself. Working with my hands and working with living, growing things got me back down to earth, so to speak, and gave me perspective."

Smart man. It's true that getting back down to earth, whether it's working the land or walking the land, can immerse us in what's good about life on earth instead of what's bad. As the *Chorus Line* lyric implies, everything is marvelous in the mountains, everything is fantastic in the forest, everything is lovely at the lake.

Art Buchwald once quipped about a political leader, "I worship the quicksand he walks on." Forget that. Worship the ground *you* walk on and resolve to immerse yourself in and appreciate earth's pleasures instead of allowing a bully to take up residence in your heart and head.

Action Plan and Discussion Questions

Is there someone in your life you're tempted to hate? Who is that person and why are you filled with resentment toward him or her? _____
_____
_____

Do you understand that hate and bad-mouthing serve no one? Can you resolve to trust that things will work out and that the people involved in this situation will figure the truth out on their own? Explain. _____
_____
_____

How are you going to immerse yourself in earthly pleasures so you focus on beauty instead of the bully? _____
_____
_____

Summary

HARMFUL BELIEFS/BEHAVIORS	HELPFUL BELIEFS/BEHAVIORS
Bad-mouth the bully and give him/her a tongue-lashing	Practice Tongue Glue and refuse to disparage the bully in public
"I'm going to let everyone know what this jerk did to me."	*"They'll only think badly of me if I bad-mouth the bully."*

Set the record straight so people know who's to blame
"They've got to understand that she's the one responsible for this."

Trust that people will figure it out on their own
"I'm going to take the high road and hope the truth will come out someday."

Bullies shroud us in their black mood
"I'm not sure I can go on. The future looks so bleak."

We surround ourselves with beauty to block out the beast
"I'm going to the concert to immerse my mind in beautiful music."

Plotting retaliation
"I'm going to get her back. She's going to be sorry she did this."

Plotting our garden
"I'm going to spend all day putting those flowers in."

Way 28. Screw Up Your Courage

Life expands or contracts in proportion to one's courage.
—ANAÏS NIN

YOU MAY BE SAYING, "OKAY, I'VE READ ALL THIS AND I AGREE WITH it; I just don't know if I have the courage to do it."

Fair enough. This chapter will show how people just like you have been in similarly daunting situations and have overcome their fear and taken action to improve their lives, and how you can, too.

As one woman suggested, she wished she had screwed up her courage to confront the bully at the time instead of feeling like she screwed up because she hadn't.

271

Don't Deflate When Subjected to Public Pressure

*How many are silenced, how many women never find their voice,
because they would have to scream?*
—ANN CLARK

A woman had gone on a skiing vacation with her family. A blizzard had wiped out all but the last afternoon of skiing, so they bustled up to the slopes to try to get in a few runs. While they were renting their equipment, their youngest daughter confided she was nervous because it had been several years since she had skied and she didn't remember how to stop. The woman reassured her daughter that a couple of trips down the bunny hill would bring her confidence back and she seemed satisfied.

Unfortunately, by the time they waited in long lines to rent equipment, they had less than two hours on the slopes. She explained to her husband that their ten-year-old wanted to get her ski legs back on the bunny hill first. Her husband replied angrily, "We don't have time for that. She can go up to the top with me and I'll teach her how on the way down."

Her daughter looked at the mother with wide, frightened eyes. The wife tried to reason with her husband: "This is her first time on skis in quite a while, and she needs at least one chance to practice her stops and turns." Her husband turned on her and raised his voice in a threatening manner. "Don't you trust me? Don't you think I know what I'm doing?"

The woman tried once more with "It will take only fifteen minutes and she'll feel better about going up." The man was livid at this point. He leaned into her, his face red and angry, and said, "I've been skiing for thirty years! Do you think I'd put my daughters in danger? You're overprotecting them again!"

At this point, both daughters were looking at her with a

mixture of fear, embarrassment, and dread. People in the area were starting to stare, so the woman caved in to avoid a scene. She patted her frightened daughter on her arm, told her it would be okay, and sent her off . . . with her daughter's look of hopeless betrayal carved in her heart.

Two hours later, the last skiers had come down and her husband and daughters had still not shown up. She searched the lodge and the ski racks. She walked back to the car and checked the lodge again, thinking she had somehow missed them. They were nowhere to be found. It started to get dark, and the ski patrol mounted up and headed up the hill. In desperation, she went to the first aid office and her worst fears were confirmed. There had been an "incident" on the mountain and her daughter was being brought down the hill on a ski sled.

Thankfully, her daughter was not seriously injured. In fact, she had had a mysterious "fall" shortly after getting off the lift, had developed hypothermia, and was unable to continue. The ski patrol brought her down mostly for safety reasons.

This woman never did confront her husband over the issue because it was "in the past, and getting upset with him after the fact wouldn't have changed what happened." She did get upset with herself, though. Her failure to stand up to her husband and for her daughter could have resulted in a tragedy. It was not her daughter's responsibility to stand up to a grown man— it was hers. She had been so intimidated by her husband and so afraid of making a scene that she had given in instead of protecting her daughter from his bullying.

She said, "In retrospect, I realize how afraid of him I was. I was afraid of his anger; I was afraid of him turning on me; I was afraid of him ridiculing me. No matter how miserably he behaved, I always tried to smooth things over and keep the peace. And my daughter almost paid the price for my unwillingness to stand up to him. That was my wake-up call."

Cause a Scene, Lest You Not Be Heard

Where people possess no authority, their rights obtain no respect.
—GEORGE BANCROFT

Remember the old adage "Children are to be seen and not heard?" That's what bullies want their partners to do. They want us to look good, quietly go along with their program, and kowtow to their authority. If we ever question their judgment, they often intentionally escalate their behavior in an effort to embarrass us so we'll back down in order to prevent a scene.

Forget that. *Make a scene!* Say, "You're darn right I don't trust you. Not when your ten-year-old daughter is telling you she's scared and you're not listening. She is going to practice on the bunny hill first so she can get her confidence back, and you are going to *back off!*"

If he gets louder in an attempt to cause you to cave and attacks with, "I know ten times more about skiing than you'll ever know," interrupt and get louder and in his face and say, "Then you know that no one should go down a slope they're not ready for." Then disengage and take charge of the situation by doing what you're going to do. Go with your daughter to the rope tow or the chair lift and don't look at the bully.

The key to causing a scene so you will be heard is to say what you're going to say and then *exit*. If you stay in a bully's vicinity, he will feel honor-bound to salve his ego and reassert his authority by continuing to bluster. Once you've said your piece, leave. This allows him to save face—he can mutter and harrumph and appear to have the last word—but you're not around to hear it.

I can't say this strongly enough. *Be willing to cause a scene.* If you don't, the manipulator in your life will know how to get the best of you. He or she will wait until you're around people and then purposely bait you because he or she knows you don't have the stomach to verbally duke it out when others are watching.

Ask yourself, "Am I going to let this individual continue to mess with my mind? Am I going to be more concerned about what people think or with making sure my rights and the rights of loved ones are respected? Am I going to allow this person to put me and my loved ones at risk because I'm afraid what bystanders might think?"

Remember, you're not causing the scene anyway. The bully is causing the scene—and you're just responding in a way to prevent him or her from doing it again.

Seldom Scene

> It is seldom that one parts on good terms, because if
> one were on good terms one would not part.
> —MARCEL PROUST

A man said, "I can really relate to this. I was aware that my wife had grown increasingly resentful of the bond between my young daughters and me, but I had no idea how bad it was until we went on vacation to Disney World. Our first day, we were waiting in the hotel lobby for the shuttle bus and I had to use the rest room. When I came out, I heard my daughters and my wife singing a little ditty. I wasn't able to hear it so, curious, I asked my daughter to sing it for me. She sang, 'Daddy's going away and he's never coming back, Daddy's going away and he's never coming back.'

"Aghast, I looked at her and asked, 'Where did you learn that?' Looking warily at her mother, she said, 'Mom taught it to us. We sing it all the time whenever you go to the bathroom.'

"Stricken, I turned to my wife, who quickly tried to do some damage control. 'It's just a joke. Don't make such a big deal about it.' 'A joke?' I squawked. 'I don't think that's very funny.'

"My wife went on the offensive at this point and tried to make me the bad guy, 'Come on, you're upsetting the girls. It was nothing.' I pressed, 'I can't believe you would teach them something like that.' Pretending to be the voice of reason, she said, 'Come on, it's our vacation. Don't ruin today by over-reacting. Let's just put it behind us and have a good time.'

"My girls were visibly distraught, looking back and forth at us and obviously fearing their big day was going to turn into a disaster. At the time I decided they shouldn't have to pay for their mother's gamesmanship, so I swallowed my pride and my indignation, and we set off for our 'fun' visit to Disney World.

"In retrospect, I wish I had said, 'Girls, we *are* going to go to Disney World today, but first we're going back to our room so your mom and I can have a talk.' I wish I had read my wife the riot act and told her in no uncertain terms that what she did was *terrible*, that she was endangering our daughter's sense of security by using them as pawns, and that she better *never* do something like that again.

"In reality, I did nothing, and I realize now that my backing down in that situation led to even more underhanded ploys to ruin my bond with my daughters."

Get Out, Get Out . . . Wherever You Are

> I stayed because I thought things would get
> better, or at least not worse.
> —FRAN BENEDETTO, MAIN CHARACTER IN
> ANNA QUINDLEN'S NOVEL *BLACK AND BLUE*

Bullies specialize in this type of diabolical, double-bind maneu-vering. They pen you in by pulling something like this and then making it seem like you're being unreasonable if you react. The movie *What's Love Got to Do with It?* tells the story of Ike and Tina Turner, as played by Lawrence Fishburne and Angela Bassett. It is probably the best depiction of the abuse cycle I've ever seen.

Outsiders often offer simplistic, stereotypic solutions to abusive relationships. They say, "Why doesn't he/she just leave? S/he must have low self-esteem."

Well, it's more complex than that, and this movie (now on video) does a wonderful job revealing the insidiousness of this type of "holy acrimony." It shows:

- the male's initial charming courtship of the woman he "must have"
- the male's growing resentment of the woman who is outshining him and no longer treating him as the alpha male
- the male's smoldering rage, which erupts with his hitting her in an effort to "beat the sass" out of this woman, who is, in his mind, emasculating him
- how hard the female tries to please him in an effort to recapture the love they once had—or at least to salvage the marriage
- how hard the female tries to appease him to keep his volatile temper at bay
- knock-down-drag-out fights, after which life "goes back to normal" and everyone acts as if nothing has happened— because both of them wish it hadn't
- the female making public and private excuses for why her lover is hitting her: "He's under a lot of pressure." "No one understands him." "It's those drugs."
- a failed escape by the woman, who is punished when she's caught, which makes her feel even more trapped and helpless
- friends and family grow increasingly concerned and frustrated with their futile attempts to convince their loved one to leave
- the reluctance of the woman to "walk out" and abandon the partner she shares so much history with and has years invested in

- the mitigating factors (public performances, record contracts, etc.) that make splitting a logistical nightmare and daunting prospect
- how the woman finally reaches her breaking point and starts fighting back. She pays a price, but at this point, she doesn't care.
- how the female starts regaining personal strength through her faith (in this case, Buddhism)
- the woman reconnecting with friends, which gives her perspective about how awful her life is, which gives her the courage to get away for good
- the man's efforts to win her back—and how quickly his sweet-talk cajoling turns into angry abuse when she rebuffs him
- a penultimate scene in which the man bluffs his way into her dressing room the night she is to star at the Ritz. He takes out a gun and threatens her. Meeting his eyes, she shows no fear and tells him to go ahead and do what he's going to do.
- the man's befuddlement when he realizes he can no longer wield his influence with her—because he has none. He's the one with the gun, but he's powerless because she's no longer afraid of him.
- the woman going on to lead a successful life as her own person

Get Away for Good

The turning point in the process of growing up is when
you discover the core of strength within you
that survives all the hurt.
—MAX LERNER

This particular film happened to be about a male abuser and a female victim; however, gender was not the point. What was so insightfully depicted was the roller-coaster world of abuse and the triumphant courage of the victim when she finally discovers the strength to get out of the situation. If you are ready to end an abusive relationship, consider the following suggestions. Hopefully, they'll help you get away for good.

1. **PLAN YOUR ESCAPE.** You wouldn't leave for a vacation without planning. Don't leave your relationship without planning. Can you save or set aside money so you'll be financially secure? Can you set up living arrangements in advance so you and your children (if you have any) will be safe? Is it feasible to kick him or her out instead of being forced to vacate your home? If you have to act on the spur of the moment, that may be better than nothing. However, it's in your best interests to think things through so your actions are wise, not rash.

2. **DON'T BE LURED BACK.** This individual will probably do everything in his/her power to woo you back. Don't be tricked by this temporary kindness. Abusers can be master manipulators who can act however they need to in order to retrap you. They may even be sincerely apologetic, but that doesn't necessarily mean things are going to change. Being sorry isn't enough. What tangible steps is he or she taking to address issues?

3. **COUNT ON TOUGH TIMES.** No one said this was going to be easy. Asking for favors is anathema for many of us. We hate to "put people out." Now is the time to lean on others and graciously accept offers of assistance. "Yes, I'll come live with you. Yes, I will take you up on your offer of a loan." As my sister learned during a bout with breast cancer, if we don't let our friends help us in our time of need, they feel helpless. Let loved ones do for you—they want to help.

4. REMIND YOURSELF OF THE BAD TIMES SO YOU DON'T WAFFLE.
The mind doesn't remember pain. A woman I know swears this forgetfulness is God's way of making sure women will be willing to go through labor again. Once we're out of an abusive situation, we tend to gloss over the really awful parts. The mind simply doesn't want to believe that such cruelty exists. Over time, we grow literally and figuratively distant from the terror of that time—which can be dangerous because it sets up the "it wasn't so bad" scenario. Normally, we don't want to dwell on hurtful incidents, but in this case it's important to remember how bad it was so you're not tempted to waver.

5. REMEMBER, THERE IS *NO* EXCUSE FOR ABUSE. Keep your Clarity Rules with you. Frequently remind yourself that you are pulling a Tina Turner and are taking responsibility for your life. Since the other person won't change, you must.

6. CONSULT A MENTAL HEALTH PROFESSIONAL. If your car breaks down, you'd take it in to a repair shop. If your toilet won't work, you'd call in a plumber. If your heart is broken and your head is spinning, schedule an appointment with a professional who has been trained to deal with matters of the heart and head. Samuel Goldwyn once quipped, "Anyone who goes to see a psychiatrist ought to have his head examined." Anyone who *doesn't* go to see a mental health professional after going ten rounds with a bully ought to have his or her head examined. Please see the Resource Directory for suggestions about books, Web sites, and support groups who can give you solid advice that will help you regain your mental footing.

7. TAKE STEPS TO ENSURE YOUR PHYSICAL, FINANCIAL, AND LEGAL SAFETY. This is not a good time to be naive. An attorney friend said, "I wish I had a hundred bucks for every person seeking a divorce who told me, 'It's not about the money.' I tell them, 'That's a noble thought. I understand that, right now, all you're thinking about is getting out of this relationship. I understand that you're not greedy and you don't want to retaliate; you just want to get away from this destructive individual.'

"And then I tell them, 'It *better* be about the money. A year from now, who is going to pay health insurance, life insurance, and dental insurance? Who's going to furnish the house, pay for college, buy the clothes? Who's going to provide for your children if something happens to you?' I tell them I know a divorced fifty-year-old woman who's had a painful abscessed tooth for months because she doesn't have the money to get it fixed. I tell them they better do their research and find a *strong* attorney who can hold his or her own going up against a snake who will manipulate the system and play dirty tricks. I suggest they sit down with a financial planner who will open their eyes as to what their financial future will be like as a single person or parent. The time to think about all this is *before* you try to get out of the relationship, not after. I'm not trying to scare them; I'm just giving them a reality check."

Take the Initiative

A lot of people never use their initiative because
nobody ever tells them to.
—COFFEE MUG SLOGAN

Don't wait for somebody to tell you what to do. Take action so you and your loved ones are no longer suffering at the hands of a bully.

One woman said, "It looks like the only option you're giving us is to end the relationship. What if we don't want to end the relationship? What if we still love this person or want to try to keep the family together?"

If it's your choice to stay with this person, then resolve to use the techniques in this book to even out the balance of power. Keep the Rights/Needs Seesaw in mind so you are more aware of bully behavior that is designed to keep you down and out. Rein in your desire to please and use your "No" power. Cut 'em off with "What did you just say to me?" if they start in with their demands and demeans. Put your hand up and "Do the You" to keep them from encroaching on your physical or emotional space. Keep your Clarity Rules and touchstone nearby to give yourself the strength of your conviction to be brave.

Action Plan and Discussion Questions

Are you trying to summon the courage to get out of an unhealthy relationship? What are some of your fears? _____
_____
_____

Do you have someone in your life who puts you in a double bind in public because they know you'll give in rather than make a scene? Who is that person? Describe a time they did this. _____
_____
_____
_____

Are you prepared to hold this person accountable from now on, even if it does mean making a big deal about it in public?
_____
_____

Can you relate to what happened in the movie *What's Love Got to Do with It?* Have any of those things happened to you? Explain. _____

_____

_____

_____

Are you ready to "pull a Tina Turner" and garner the courage to get out of an unhealthy relationship and take charge of your life? How so? _____

_____

_____

_____

Summary

HARMFUL BELIEFS/BEHAVIORS	HELPFUL BELIEFS/BEHAVIORS
Deflate when bully puts us in double bind *"I don't want to be a spoilsport, so I'll go to the family reunion."*	Determined to hold bully accountable for double bind *"One more word out of you and I'm not going to the reunion."*
Manipulator pressures us into going along because we don't want to make a scene *"You don't want to put your mom at risk with her bad heart and all."*	Willing to make a scene so the bully doesn't get away with this ploy *"No, Mom, things aren't all right. Aaron hit me last night."*

Bully puts us on defensive by demanding, "Don't you trust me?"
"Come on, you don't want to upset everybody at Christmas dinner. Trust me on this."

Focus on the issue, which is they're not behaving in a way that deserves trust
"I will do what I think is best and I want them to know it's over between us."

Abusive cycle continues with armed peace, escalation of anger, eruption, temporary remorse and honeymoon, armed peace, etc.
"He promised he wouldn't hit me again. It wasn't really his fault, he's worried about work."

Break out of abusive cycle by leaving relationship or by abuser agreeing to get professional help
"If we start counseling this week, I'll consider a trial separation instead."

React with empty threat
"You shouldn't have said that. You're going to make me mad."

Respond with responsible action
"I have a restraining order and you are to stay away from me."

Summary and Action Plan: Saviour Self— The Buck Starts Here

I plan on living forever. So far, so good.
—Coffee mug slogan

DON'T YOU JUST LOVE THE ABOVE QUOTE? IT'S A WONDERFUL reminder that, no matter what's happening, we're alive, which means there's plenty to be grateful for. As Maurice Chevalier said, "Old age isn't so bad when you consider the alternative." Dealing with a bully can be bad news, but as along as we're alive, free, and learning, we still have alternatives and hopes of better days ahead.

Don't Wait to Be Rescued

I like things to happen; and if they don't happen,
I like to make them happen.
—Sir Winston Churchill

The primary message of this book is that as bad as things may be, there are still specific steps you can take to take back your life. The message is also that *you* need to take these steps because the situation won't improve by itself. The proverbial white knight won't come in and save the day. You are the only one who can save this day. As has been said before, this may not be your fault, but it is your responsibility.

American short-story writer O. Henry said, "Life is made up of sobs, sniffles, and smiles, with sniffles predominating." I disagree. I believe the proportion of sobs, sniffles, and smiles in our life is up to us. On any given day, there might be cause for all three. The question is, Which will we allow to dominate and direct our thinking?

Have you learned from this individual? Are you stronger? Are you clearer about who you are and how you want to be in this world? Are you more appreciative of what's right in your life? Has this nightmare revealed your real friends to you? Have you been comforted by the support of strangers? Will the lessons you've learned serve you the rest of your days?

Then this experience has served a purpose, hasn't it? You've emerged, or can emerge, from this ordeal, with strength, wisdom, and a renewed appreciation for loving individuals who act with integrity.

Make Music with What's Left

> Those who follow the part of themselves that is great will become great. Those that follow the part that is small will become small.
> —MENCIUS

There is a wonderful story about the gifted violinist Itzhak Perlman who gave a memorable concert at Avery Fisher Hall at Lincoln Center in New York City. Perlman was stricken with polio as a child; as a result, he has braces on both legs and walks with the aid of two crutches. Perlman is a shining example of an individual who has followed and developed the parts of him that are great. He is universally respected for his talent and poise under pressure, which were magnificently demonstrated on this particular evening.

After laboriously making his way onto the stage, Perlman had settled into his chair and started warming up, when one of his violin strings broke. People in the audience thought he would probably have to go through the complicated process of leaving the stage to find another violin or replace the string, but he did neither. Instead, he collected himself for a moment, and then motioned for the conductor and orchestra to begin playing.

Jack Reimer of the *Houston Chronicle*, who reported what happened, said, "Of course, anyone knows that it is impossible to play a symphonic work with just three strings. I know that, and you know that, but that night Itzhak Perlman refused to know that. You could see him modulating, changing, recomposing the piece in his head, getting new sounds from the strings they had never made before."

When Perlman finished, there was initial silence and then everyone in the room rose in a spontaneous standing ovation, wildly cheering his extraordinary performance. In response to the appreciative applause, Perlman said simply, "You know, sometimes it is the artist's task to find out how much music you can still make with what you have left."

Know that you still have music left to play, and it is time to get on your way.

Travel the Highway of Hope

"How do you find your way back in the dark?" "Just head for that big star straight on. The highway's under it, takes us right home."
—Arthur Miller

I always wait to write the last chapter until, well . . . the last minute. That may sound like a blazing attack of the obvious;

however, it's my way of leaving room for serendipity. Writing a book can take up to a year and a lot can happen over the course of finishing a manuscript. I got to the last chapter today, and lo and behold, a letter arrived in the mail from a man I've never met. He had just finished reading my *ConZentrate* book and was moved to write from where he's living . . . in prison. He writes:

> *I was pacing around the cell, which is my usual habit at six-thirty in the morning, or roughly whatever time it is, and I started staring out the window and watching the sunrise. I was sitting there quietly concentrating on my breathing and I had an epiphany and decided to write what occurred to me. And it was this:*

> *If you look out the window—you see the fence.*
> *If you look past the fence—you see the gate.*
> *If you look past the gate—you see the grass.*
> *If you look past the grass—you see the horizon.*
> *If you look past the horizon—you see the dawn.*
>   *That's because the sun is coming up.*

> *I don't know if your book inspired me or just had me in a creative train of mind, but I thought this might help someone. I look at it like this: I'm in prison possibly for the rest of my life, and if I can get out of my funk and see the sunrise, someone that is out in the real world should be able to look up and find the sun in their life. If you can use this letter to help others, then it's my greatest pleasure that I took the time to do it. That's really all I wanted to say.*

Nice Recovery

Valor consists in the power of self-recovery.
—RALPH WALDO EMERSON

Thank you, Joshua. He's right. If you are imprisoned in an unhealthy relationship with someone who is trying to fence you in, take steps to free yourself from this person who is trying to lock you in and rob you of your independence.

If you'll look back to the opening pages of this book, you'll find that it is dedicated to people who are being, or have been, targeted by a bully. I hope this book has helped you develop the courage, clarity, and communication skills to recover a more meaningful, satisfying life. I know there is a better future waiting for you. The sun is shining as I write this, and it will shine for you too if you'll take your bully by the horns and take back your life. Best wishes, and, as Arthur Miller so eloquently suggested, travel the highway of hope.

Action Plan and Discussion Questions

Are you ready to live and learn? Do you believe that you can extract value from this experience so it actually serves you? Explain. _____

_____

_____

Are you clear that you will "saviour self" and not wait to be rescued? What action are you going to take today to take back control of your life? _____

_____

_____

Think back over the book. What is one specific suggestion that was particularly insightful or helpful for you? _____

_____

_____

What is one thing you're going to do differently from now on when you encounter someone who is crossing the line with unfair behavior? _____

_____

_____

What is one piece of advice you would give someone else if they are dealing with a bully? _____

_____

_____

How are you going to remind yourself to stay strong? Are you going to take your soft rock with you, copy the Clarity Rules and post them where you can keep them in sight and in mind, or what?_____

_____

_____

Resource Directory

COMEDIENNE LILY TOMLIN SAID, TONGUE FIRMLY PLANTED IN cheek, "Remember, we're all in this . . . alone." Thankfully, we don't have to deal with bullies all by our lonesome. There are support groups, Web sites, and books available to help us deal with individuals who are doing their best to control, manipulate, or abuse us.

Please pick up the phone, stop by your favorite library or bookstore, or log on the Internet today to seek out information and individuals who can help you minimize the damage caused by destructive people. They are there to help. Let them.

RECOMMENDED BOOKS

Building Confidence/Courage/Assertiveness

Maria Arapakis. *Softpower! How to Speak Up, Set Limits, and Say No Without Losing Your Lover, Your Job, or Your Friends.* New

York: Warner Books, 1990. This book is more than a decade old, but its tips are timeless. Discover for yourself why best-selling author M. Scott Peck said this book is "a wise and balanced book on healthy personal power." Practical suggestions and interesting stories show how to stick up for your opinions, make tough decisions when pressured, stand up to hotheads, and say yes only when you mean it.

Sam Horn. *What's Holding You Back? Thirty Days to Having the Courage and Confidence to Do What You Want, Meet Whom You Want, and Go Where You Want.* New York: St. Martin's Press, 1997. *Way of the Peaceful Warrior* author Dan Millman said, "Step-by-step practical advice, like that of a wise and supportive friend, reminding us all of who we are and what we're capable of." The sections on Control (Know What You Stand For and What You Won't Stand For) and Courage (Face and Erase Your Fears) are particularly helpful if you're dealing with someone who is trying to intimidate or manipulate you.

Anne Katherine. *Where to Draw the Line.* New York: Fireside Books, 2000. A newer work by the author of the classic book *Boundaries: Where You End and I Begin.* No-nonsense language and many examples make this an interesting and useful read for anyone who has a history of giving in to go along. This is a short book that is easy to dip into even if you have only a few minutes to spare.

Bullying on the Job

Noa Davenport, Ruth D. Schwartz, Gail P. Elliott, and Sabra Vidali. *Mobbing: Emotional Abuse in the American Workplace.* Ames, Iowa: Civil Society Publishing, 1999. Check out the testimonials for this book on www.Amazon.com. Many grateful readers have thanked the authors for uncovering and articulating the insidious ostracizing they experienced in their jobs. If you feel "ganged up on" at work, check out this book.

Susan Herman Magriet Marais. *Corporate Hyenas at Work.* Johannesburg: Kagiso Publishers, 1997. In South Africa, they call bullying "mobbing," and this book explains how to deal with corporate hostilities and aggression no matter what shape they take. Packed with success stories of readers who put these ideas into practice.

Gary and Ruth Namie. *The Bully at Work: What You Can Do to Stop the Hurt and Reclaim Your Dignity on the Job.* Naperville, Ill.: Sourcebooks, Inc., 2000. This text is packed with case studies, recent research and statistics, and many practical suggestions on how to address workplace violence. The Namies are the pioneers of the Campaign Against Workplace Bullying, which seeks to uncover and cure the silent "bully" epidemic that devastates the lives, careers, and families of millions.

Abusive Relationships/Domestic Violence

Kay Douglas. *Invisible Wounds: A Self-Help Guide for Women in Destructive Relationships.* The Women's Press, 1996. This book has the ring of truth because the author draws on her own experience and that of more than fifty women to demonstrate how to recognize, resolve, and recover from emotional abuse.

Beverly Engel. *The Emotionally Abused Woman: Overcoming Destructive Patterns and Reclaiming Yourself.* New York: Fawcett Books, 1992. If you feel unfairly criticized or put upon in your life, you're going to relate to this book. Many therapists recommend it because it clearly points out how we sometimes unintentionally contribute to others taking advantage of us—and explains how we can start standing up for ourselves.

Patricia Evans. *The Verbally Abusive Relationship: How to Recognize It and How to Respond.* Adams Media, 1992. Thousands and thousands of women say they owe their sanity to this author and her groundbreaking book. There could be no finer endorsement of this book than to click on to www.Amazon.com and read the dozens of heartfelt letters from readers who say this book saved their life. Many women in my seminars have said they dog-eared every page because they recognized themselves and the verbally abusive person in their life in every situation she describes. The beauty of this book is, not only does it explain why abusers do what they do, it outlines how to put a stop to it. Highly recommended.

Susan Forward and Joan Torres. *Men Who Hate Women and the Women Who Love Them: When Loving Hurts and You Don't Know Why.* New York: Bantam, 1987. A classic in this field. This author is one of the country's leading advocates for women developing the clarity and confidence to be only in healthy relationships. Her later books, *Emotional Blackmail, Toxic Parents,* and *Toxic In-Laws* are also full of real-life examples so readers can learn techniques that have worked successfully for others.

Pamela Jayne. *Ditch That Jerk: Dealing with Men Who Control and Hurt Women.* Alameda, Calif.: Hunter House, 2000. Although this book focuses on dealing with men who are abusive (or on the brink of being abusive), gender is not the point. The value of this book lies in the fact that the author does a good job of identifying the warning signs of "utterly hopeless" individuals so we can avoid getting into relationships with someone who is only going to cause harm.

Mary Susan Miller. *No Visible Wounds.* New York: Fawcett, 1996. The subtitle of this book is "Identifying Nonphysical

Abuse of Women by Their Men." However, the book is full of excellent insights and advice about all types of controlling, tyrannical behavior, regardless of gender.

Noelle Nelson. *Dangerous Relationships: How to Stop Domestic Violence Before It Stops You.* New York: Perseus Publishing, 1997. A bounty of practical tips on how to spot, prevent, and correct unhealthy behaviors before they jeopardize your emotional health. The personalized Safety Plan (intended to enable you to think through what you should do if physically threatened) at the end of the book is worth the price of the whole book.

Ginny Nicarthy. *Getting Free: You Can End Abuse and Take Back Your Life.* New York: Seal Press, 1997. Ingram Booksellers says this is "a most important work in the movement to end domestic violence." The emphasis is on freeing yourself from destructive relationships so you can lead the life you were meant to lead.

Lucy Papillon. *When Hope Can Kill: Reclaiming Your Soul in a Romantic Relationship.* Nashville, Tenn.: Everywhere Press, 1998. This book has a very important message—hope can sometimes be our worst enemy. This book offers practical alternatives to wishing things would get better. It shows how to develop the strength to dissolve damaging relationships.

Dealing with "Ordinary" Difficult People

C. Leslie Charles. *Why Is Everyone So Cranky? The Ten Trends Complicating Our Lives and What We Can Do About Them.* New York: Hyperion, 2001. As endorser Michael LeBoeuf, author of *Working Smart,* said, "It is a problem of epidemic proportion and a question begging for an answer: If we are doing so well, why are so many people so rude?" The author's brilliant book offers many strategies for reversing aggravation and irritability in ourselves and others.

Thomas Crum. *The Magic of Conflict: Turning a Life of Work into a Work of Art.* New York: Touchstone, 1987. This pioneering work is based on Aikido, a Japanese martial art and mind-body discipline. It provides a variety of ways to turn conflict into a chance to change, and shows how struggle can lead to success—if we approach it with the right mind-set and tools.

Sam Horn. *Tongue Fu!® How to Deflect, Disarm, and Defuse Any Verbal Conflict.* New York: St. Martin's Press, 1996. *Executive Book Summaries* said, "This book is a gold mine for anyone who deals with the public. The author has added to the legacy of ideas on dealing with people left by Abraham Lincoln, Benjamin Franklin, Dale Carnegie, and many others." The focus is on how we can communicate in ways that turn conflicts into cooperation.

Les Parrott III. *The Control Freak: Coping with Those Around You. Taming the One Within.* Wheaton, Ill.: Tyndale House Publishers, 2001. This book offers suggestions on how to deal with individuals who have to be in charge at all costs—whether that person is yourself or someone else.

Douglas Stone, Bruce Patton, and Shelia Heen. *Difficult Conversations: How to Discuss What Matters Most.* New York: Penguin, 2000. *Fast Company* magazine called this "a user-friendly guide to mastering the talks we dread . . . a keeper." One of the most important points the authors make is that we're imperfect. Once we accept that, we no longer feel so defensive or fragile about our faults, which makes us less vulnerable to manipulators' attempts to knock us off balance.

HOTLINES TO LINK YOU WITH SUPPORT
GROUPS/ASSISTANCE

Don't know where to turn? Are you and your loved ones at risk? Have you looked through the yellow pages and you don't know how to contact a shelter or protective agency? Would you like to talk with someone who understands your situation?

The following hotlines can be reached with a confidential phone call, twenty-four hours a day, seven days a week. The hotline staff can provide victims and those calling on their behalf with crisis intervention. They have an up-to-date list of programs and services in your area, including counselors, support groups, and legal information. Many have emergency shelters or other housing options.

All hotlines strictly protect the anonymity of anyone who seeks their services, so you don't have to worry about the bully or any of his friends/family finding out about your call or visit. The phone call and many of their services are free of charge to everyone. If you want help and aren't sure how to get it, call these numbers.

- **National Domestic Violence Hotline:** 1-800-799-7233 (SAFE) (for the hearing impaired): 1-800-787-3224
- **National Organization for Victim Assistance Hotline:** 1-800-870-6682

HELPFUL WEB SITES

www.TakeTheBullyByTheHorns.com
This Web site is an outgrowth of this book and my seminars on this topic. Visit it monthly for new articles, quizzes, media appearances, and tips on how to prevent people from running and ruining your life.

www.bullyfreeworld.com
This Web site features recent research and strategies on this topic, and describes the anti-bullying programs the sponsors hold in schools and institutions.

www.bullying.co.uk
This Web site is based in Great Britain, but its information is universally applicable. It offers pages and pages of information on new policies in schools (including the controversial no-blame approach). It shares results from recent surveys on bullying and isn't afraid to tackle political hot potatoes.

www.bullybeware.com
This Web site, based in British Columbia, Canada, reports recent media stories on bullying, and takes the approach that teachers, students, support staff, parents, and administrators need to work as a team to take action against bullying.

www.apeacemaker.net
This Web site is dedicated to documenting community conflict resolution efforts that are taking place around the globe. The sponsors of the Web site, the Network of Communities for Peacemaking and Conflict Resolution, believe that educating people about the value of cooperation and showcasing events where people get along peacefully will help to increase our ability to get along.

www.acresolution.org
This Web site is a result of several professional organizations bonding together to create the Association for Conflict Resolution. Their mission is to enhance and promote the practice and public understanding of peaceful, effective conflict resolution. The site features a Learning Center, Products and Services, a Community Center, Conferences and Programs, and a Dialogue and Feedback chat room.

www.bullybusters.org
This site is sponsored by Gary and Ruth Namie, founders of the Campaign Against Workplace Bullying, whose mission is to offer self-education, research, and advocacy for reform for people whose health and careers have been or are being injured by psychological violence at work. This helpful site not only describes the origins and effects of bully behavior, it describes how you can help change the laws in your state so you can stamp out bully behavior.

www.amazon.com
Enter Bully in the search engine to bring up a complete list of the newest and most popular books on bullying in school, in the workplace, and in relationships. The editorial reviews and reader reviews can give you a good idea of whether a particular book would be relevant and helpful for you.

We Want to Hear from You

Did this book help you resolve a situation with a challenging person in your life? Were you able to successfully deal with a bully—without becoming one yourself?

We'd love to hear your success stories. With your permission, we'd like to share them on our Web site www.TakeThe-BullyByTheHorns.com or in a future book or seminar so others might benefit from your insights and experience.

Do you have a bully dilemma that wasn't covered in this book? Please get in touch. We update our Web site frequently and would love to address your question in one of our upcoming newsletters or feature articles.

Are you interested in arranging or attending a "Take the Bully by the Horns" presentation? Sam Horn was the top-rated speaker at both the 1996 and 1998 International Platform Association conventions and has given presentations for such clients as Hewlett-Packard, the IRS, the U.S. Navy, and the National Governors Association. She offers action-packed seminars full of real-life ideas your participants will be inspired to put into use immediately at work, at home, at school, and in the community.

Please contact Cheri Grimm at the address below to arrange for Sam to keynote your next convention, provide training for your employees, or present a program for your school. Cheri will be glad to answer your questions and schedule Sam to address your next meeting.

Take the Bully by the Horns Seminars
Attn. Cheri Grimm
P.O. Box 6810
Los Osos, CA 93402
Phone 805-528-4351
Fax 805-528-2581
E-mail: info@samhorn.com
Web site: www.samhorn.com